# 1000 Words
# Photobook Conversations

# Introduction:
## *Photobook Ecosystems*
## Duncan Wooldridge

*Duncan Wooldridge is an artist, writer and curator, and is Reader in Photography at the School of Digital Arts, Manchester School of Art, Manchester Metropolitan University. He is the author of* John Hilliard: Not Black and White *(Ridinghouse, 2014),* To Be Determined: Photography and the Future *(SPBH Editions, 2021) and Co-Editor of* Writer Conversations *(1000 Words, 2023).*

The production of photographic images is rarely a solitary activity. It is not that the making of an image can never be carried out alone: it might be produced on the fly, within personal space, without notice or never broadcasted. But for most photographers and artists and many other cultural producers alike, the large production of a body of work not only involves collaborating with many others – using the tools of manufacturers and fabricators, and working with professional printers, designers, editors, curators, galleries and bookstores, archivists and critics, historians, and researchers – but it is made to be shared. It is also only one of many activities that will be carried out surrounding that work: the production of an image is never its conclusion, because the work is made to go out in the world, and how it does this and the conversations the work gives rise to contributes to many of its gestures and meanings, and its ultimate consequences. Alongside this are the economic realities of these practices: a photographer, designer or publisher is just as likely to take on work as an assistant, a producer, a facilitator, an advisor, a teacher or a salaried employee, supplementing their activities with additional funds.

Beyond or perhaps in direct defiance of that economic sphere, the image-producer does not stop there. They are just as likely to also to build for themselves an identity as an editor, a writer, a publisher or a curator, the founder of a residency programme or a system of mentorship, an organiser of workshops, a collector or a librarian or custodian – tasks which address a social need, and for which there is often a lesser, equally precarious living to be earned. Such a scope of activities might prompt a sense of exhaustion, but it begins to show how the image connects to, and operates amongst, an enlarged gamut of activities, communities and functions. Because images are significant objects and surfaces, they produce wide-ranging ramifications and programmes. Photography might seem deceptively simple on the surface, but burrow beneath this and we find so many rhizomatic interconnections and entanglements. Today, images and image-makers function as parts of elaborate ecosystems, as part of several spokes emerging out of a singular activity.

A small range of organisations and activities might illustrate this critical point: in Dhaka, Bangladesh, photographer Shahidul Alam founded not only the Drik Photo Agency, but also Pathshala South Asian Media Institute and the Chobi Mela Photo Festival. They began somewhat separately, but today occupy the same building, and produce a mix of educational programmes, generating income through

     *Duncan Wooldridge*

picture sales and public platforms for photography's dissemination. It is not uncommon for faculty at Pathshala to work at Drik or be a part of the programme team for Chobi Mela, such are their crossovers. In Tokyo, Japan, Taisuke Koyama founded Tokyo Photographic Research, a collective of artist-photographers who set out to research the transformation of the city through a series of projects, catalysed by the series of grand projects begun in the context of the Tokyo Olympics. TPR not only make their own research projects, but collaborate with businesses to produce artists commissions and exhibitions, operate an artist's studio platform and have begun a residency programme through collaborations in Switzerland and the Netherlands. In Dublin, Ireland, one of the most elaborate models of an ecosystem can be observed: PhotoIreland Festival, developed by Ángel Luis González Fernández, has grown from a biannual exhibition to include a bookstore, a regular print sales event, a commissioning platform, a mentoring project and a critical journal, whilst also collaborating to further networks including the Europe-wide FUTURES programme supporting photographers, curators and writers. It is, González Fernández says, a 360-degree support system. And this is before we have really touched upon the photobook, that most social of photographic forms.

In Berlin, Germany, in 2018, Bruno Ceschel's Self Publish, Be Happy and C/O Berlin organised the series of workshops entitled Photobook: Reset. A meeting of 30 professionals and 30 members of the public, it explored the forms and contents of the photobook, proposing that we might need to start over at a moment when the Western-European photobook bubble had deflated and the global practice of publishing was yet to be fully recognised. It was the first moment in which I met Ana Casas Broda, one of the founders of Hydra + Fotografía in Mexico City. Ana, with the designer Ramon Pez, was completing Inframundo, a vast project to publish 16 brand new photobooks by new photographers and distribute them by going to fairs and events internationally after a process of Incubadora ('*Incubator*') workshops. At one moment towards the end of the workshop in Berlin, when the inevitable question "What do we do next?" was raised across the participants, only Ana, without hesitation, said: "I'll host you all in Mexico". Nervous laughter rippled around the participants, but Ana was absolutely serious: she wanted to kickstart the next stage. The future of the photobook is going to involve a shifting awareness and new communities.

Today, a global practice of photobook publishing has become visible: diverse cultures of the photobook have emerged and a second wave of the photobook has taken hold. Today's publishing practice is decentralising territories and values. Many of its innovations are to be found not only in the visuals of the book and accompanying textual content, but in its materials and its forms of circulation: what it is made of, who it is made for and how it can be accessed. Where the book had become collectible and an object of financial speculation in the first wave, leading to an attempt to map similar riches across different continents in a series of photobook history anthologies, in the second, it is purposefully identifying a series of changing social forces and recognising a capacity to act to modify collective histories and imaginaries. Access is part of its politics: today's photobook can be affordable or small in scale, printed with local materials or made first and foremost to build or sustain a community in its own specific environs. It might be open to travel and connect, build new and diverse audiences or engage in disciplinary discourse, but not at the expense of the former. In many of these contexts, the direct and tangible politics of everyday life, including the politics of gender, sexuality, race, social and political power, capital, and inequality, privilege and colonial histories, are laid bare; for a viewer or reader accustomed to being addressed in English or presented with tightly configured visual formulae, it will at first lay down a challenge. The photobook now opens up a rich variety of new forms, new models of engagement and interaction, and with it a shifting map of the possible.

A Social Medium

If the social image, digitally networked as it is, appears to move with a frictionless abandon – one image replacing another, and another following that, without apparent beginning or end – to who and for whom does it travel? Byung-Chul Han writes, in a scathing critique of never-ending production, that, in the sphere of user-centred media, '[n]o one is *listening*; everyone is playing to the gallery.' Our contemporary audience is often everyone *and* no one. Access to broadcasting tools might be widespread, but the reception within those audiences is stratified. Recent research suggests that online videos, which have displaced much of broadcast television through platforms such as YouTube, contain a very small percentage of highly watched items alongside an overwhelming majority of those which

     *Duncan Wooldridge*

receive little to no tangible audience whatsoever (the median average views for a video on YouTube is in fact just 40 people). We have moved ever closer towards a ceaseless production – something which machine learning only extends – but our attention has certainly not extended to meet demand. This social image allows for useful contrasts to help us think about and understand the ongoing significance of the photobook because, as a discursive and equally social object, albeit one which travels with overt material and logistical constraints, its growth of new audiences suggests a challenge laid down to the social form of networked communication, or at least its overcoming. The popularisation of the photobook as a form, its popularity amongst students and emerging practitioners especially, suggests it possesses qualities that we should pay attention to.

We might reflect on the photobook by recognising that it openly speculates about its reception, however discreetly or unconsciously. The practice of publishing photobooks begins with an imagined and prospective audience. This does not exclude those who self-publish, who choose to circumvent the collaboration with a publisher (and perhaps a designer) only to enter a similar circuit of fellow makers, bookstores, fairs, commentators, and collectors. Self-publishers merely take an active role in each of these interactions where it might otherwise be shared with, or looked after by, their collaborator. Either way, the decision to publish is a making-public: it is to address an audience that is necessarily possible but which is yet to be brought about. Like its digital kin, the photobook shares an interest in sequential encounter and structure, and places an equally prominent emphasis upon storytelling to hold attention, but the outcome of whether this task of reaching out to an audience is successful is experienced very differently. This is because the digital image and the photobook are also each concerned with movement and distribution, though their methods differ starkly. Whilst the platforms for social networks are potentially large and seem readily available, they are, as we have seen, profoundly non-specific. Technology makes the act of publishing seem simple by concealing its gestures or decisions, where the production of a book reveals a series of labours and investments explicitly. In the digital, any split or focus towards an audience is made not by the producer, but by the social platform's mediating algorithm, permitting makers to retain a strange, universalising conviction that their work is for all. Digitally published images are built upon a quick moving redundancy, so they are necessarily both urgent and maximalist. By contrast, the photobook-maker or publisher has to meet the recipient halfway. They must ensure the book is made sufficiently visible, often travelling to fairs and bookstores to manually distribute many of the copies. Here, however, they recognise and shape their audience, choosing to gravitate towards economic power or smaller, potentially unknown communities of possibility. The photobook is made with a recognition of a smaller audience, returning only if demand persists. But, in turn, it may just as equally demand more time of the viewer and encourage not only a first encounter, but a review and revisiting. A striking example of this might be Gábor Gerhes' *The Atlas*, a photobook in an edition of 500 copies, exhibited at the Kiscell Museum in Budapest, Hungary, in 2022. To see *The Atlas*, a photobook that deconstructed its namesake as an encyclopaedic source of knowledge and orientation, it was necessary to climb the hill to the museum in order to travel to the book. All of the book's editions, none of which were offered for sale, could be borrowed from the shelves and browsed at reading tables, inside a distinctive and dramatic installation, developed by Gerhes with curator Emese Mucsi and architectural firm Paradigma Ariadné. The concentration that this invoked, knowing that the book would remain on the hill, was memorable and rewarding, focusing the attention of the viewer and giving them overt but nonetheless free choice to skim or to spend time. Knowledge is always situated; here, it was physically manifest.

Key questions – who is a book's audience, and to what extent is that audience necessarily local and/or global – are addressed by the act of publishing and its surrounds. Anshika Varma's Offset Projects, a publishing project with both a situated and mobile library, Pitara, which is also an initiator of discussions and workshop groups, based in New Delhi, used the moment of the pandemic to initiate Guftgu, meaning 'conversation' or 'exchange', a series of dialogues sharing knowledge, resources and the histories of photobook publishing in South Asia. Later becoming the form for an edited artist's book collecting the work of 10 photographers who had developed their work through Offset's catalysing conversation and debate, presented in their own standalone chapters, Guftgu demonstrates the layered differences with our dominant forms of communication. The rise of publishing projects which just as significantly orient themselves around the provision of resources – knowledge, skills, the sharing of objects, and a community of people with similar motivations or interests – converge around the book. However grand or philosophical

that might sound, here publishing is both a kind of community
and a form of world-making, reframing what we might think of as
sustainability not only as a response to environmental collapse,
but as the building of new ways of being concerned with dialogue
and sufficiency over endless accumulation.

This trajectory, and the artists and photographers who have
become to bookmakers, publishers, booksellers, workshop providers,
librarians, conversation starters, and ecosystem builders, gave rise
to this book and its model of collaboration. It is a balance of local
and internationally recognised knowledges, and is built upon the
collaborative work that we have each experimented with. Like any
object which attempts to observe or map an impossibly large field,
it is necessarily incomplete, but hopefully it can begin some things.

*Photobooks:*
*Context, Authorship and Education*
Ana Casas Broda

Ana Casas Broda is an artist, educator and editor based in Mexico City. She is Co-Director of Hydra + Fotografía, a platform for projects related to the medium of photography.

Photobooks bring together two things that obsess me and have been central in my life: learning processes in the field of art, and their manifestations in narratives and storytelling.

In a time eating away at certainties, if I ever had any, my ideas about the photobook are constantly mutating and transforming. Born in Granada, Spain, to a Viennese mother and an Andalusian father, I spent my first nine years being transported from one country to another depending on my parents' complicated relationship. From the age of six, my mother left for Mexico, in love with the foreign and the exotic, pursuing her career as a historian specialising in Aztec religion. For two years, I longed to follow her, and, in 1974, my father allowed me to leave. Upon arriving in Mexico, the first thing my mother did was take me on a long car ride with a renowned anthropologist and her son through indigenous villages and archaeological sites from Mexico City to Chiapas, Guatemala and finally El Salvador. Since then, my life has been formed in Mexico, with regular stays in Vienna, Austria, and Spain. My vision of the world of the photobook is marked by my life that has flowed between continents since childhood. And it has marked my professional work in this field as an artist, educator and publisher. I find it natural to create spaces where different cultures, languages, ways of conceiving and working converge. And I find them essential in raising fundamental, critical questions about the form, function and context of the photobook in contemporary society.

Mexico, with more than 68 indigenous cultures which precede the Spanish conquest, and their own languages and social structures, is a society full of layers, symbolised by the construction of the capital of New Spain literally on the pyramids of Tenochtitlan. This territory is marked by the coexistence and constant tension between mestizos, indigenous cultures and immigrants from all over the world, especially the great right-wing dictatorships of Europe and Latin America, as well as contrasting social strata. Complex and antagonistic worldviews have survived thanks to the resistance and strength of their cultures, in a fascinating and indecipherable society. It was only in the late 2000s, with the advent of the internet and the democratisation of cameras, that, in Mexico, photography began to cease being a tool of power and indigenous peoples received access to information on photography from around the world, as well as cameras. In this way, international contemporary photography amalgamates with completely different indigenous cosmovisions.

Shortly before leaving the Centro de la Imagen in Mexico City, where I had worked since 1994, we created the independent space Hydra + Fotografía. For the last seven years, I have been in charge of a Contemporary Photography Seminar, collaborating with CASA in Oaxaca, creating workshop groups which mix indigenous authors and makers with people from all over the world, particularly where there were no spaces for education in photography. I was clear that this work in formative, developmental processes was the centre of my interests. In 2016, I built the PHOTOBOOK INCUBATOR, an experimental and flexible programme that seeks to open new possibilities for the creation of photobooks. The incubator is distinctive because it provides conceptual and practical tools and diverse and contradictory voices for authors to develop their own voice and work.

Photobook Circuits

The established international photobook circuit is interesting, but it certainly does not have the capacity to sustain the needs of the medium. Books need flexible, open spaces, and, by that, I mean concrete, local, easily accessed and wider or more diverse libraries, workshops, stores, and more, to respond to all the authors who find in this medium the ways to create their work.

The production of photobooks by independent publishers is growing in Central and South America, but there is only a fragmented infrastructure to provide an outlet for them. In a continent with a large number of extraordinary photographers across several generations, only recently can we find a significant number of independent publishing projects, which in many cases also operate bookstores and/or organise photobook festivals. Significant projects (and here I can mention only a fraction) are: the library at the Instituto Moreira Salles and Lovely House in Brazil; FLACH and Casa Espacio FIFV in Chile; TURMA, Fotolibro rodante, ASUNTO IMPRESO Librería de la Imagen and the FELIFA and MIGRA fairs in Argentina; and Centro de Fotografía de Montevideo and the San José Foto Festival in Uruguay, along with many others that emerge in isolated places with independent proposals. How these can become better interconnected and sustainable is the next urgent question. For the last few years, there has been a proliferation of independent printed art fairs – not exclusively photobook fairs – with a larger audience and more propositional content.

The world of the photobook is changing at an astonishing speed. Leaving behind the classic models of European photobooks, independent projects emerge that respond to local problematics and possibilities, enriching the panorama with new visions and forms of experimentation. Nevertheless, it is important to underline that most of the initiatives that have lasted over time have support from the state. Government grants in countries such as Chile, Mexico and Uruguay play a major role in the production of the photobooks and festivals that have become visible. What is yet to emerge is a multitude of private or commercially sustainable projects. The country with the most independent bookstores and photobook fairs is Argentina, and perhaps this explains why Argentinian books are starting to appear in different countries. Zooming out, there are only a small number of dedicated photobook stores worldwide, and it is a challenge for them to balance supporting a local community with widening the reach and perceptions of their audiences. Equally, there is no genuinely viable distribution system to support books beyond the existing Western axis. Shipments between Latin American countries are so complicated that they are effectively impossible (just the same as it is with the flow to other continents), whilst being expensive and time-consuming, requiring travel grants or new systems of collaboration in order to begin the process.

The next urgent step is to change the ways in which books are produced and circulated. Proposals such as local printing of the same books in different continents, or a network that allows books to be stored in different countries, a common effort of publishers, fairs and other elements that participate in this circuit, would be key to transforming the complexity to which authors, publishers and the public are currently exposed. Across Latin America, there are spaces that do significant and valuable work for the creation, dissemination and circulation of photobooks. However, they tend to include almost exclusively participants from the region, and an exchange with other continents is not achieved.


Education and Authorship


Each author and each book needs a different process to get published. Some will be solitary works in which the author immerses themselves in a monologue that requires silence. Other times, a team is necessary to dialogue, experiment and achieve a collaborative work where the different voices are fundamental. For all of these reasons, I consider the education processes as crucial in the creation of photobooks. This must have the flexibility to help authors understand their personal needs and those of their projects, to know that there are options and that it is fundamental that they can find the way of working that allows them to develop their project in the best way. At Hydra, we are especially interested in working with authors from cultures or communities with their own worldviews that do not usually have access to conventional art circuits, with authors with politically, socially or personally relevant themes that urgently need to give shape to a work that materialises their ideas. In that sense, I consider an author someone who develops knowledge of design and writing tools, about materials and production methods, whilst assimilating this information naturally into their creative process and integrating it into the development of the book. I believe in the author as the creator of the work. The tools are part of the process of discovery, like any other artistic discipline. This does not mean that the other participants – designers and editors, amongst others – do not have an important and deeply enriching role. But by understanding the work of each of them, the author can decide how to guide the collaborative process in the way that their own process best requires.

As authors develop a critical vision of the photobook, in the economic, social and political contexts in which they are created, reflecting upon the viability of their production – the validation circuits, the audiences they wish to reach – makes the medium much more dynamic, much more challenging, and the publications much more interesting, radical and propositional. This evidently changes the medium itself. The photograph is no longer seen as a single piece, but as an articulated discourse of an author who has a coherent proposal. Given the social, political and economic panorama of the contemporary photobook in the world, it is fundamental the photobook addresses relevant, critical and urgent issues, which include the viability of production, circulation and the awareness of how economics will determine the life of the book. It seems to me that, as authors, we should give greater relevance to these aspects in the creation of photobooks. As receivers and participants in the photobook ecosystem, we should also bring this to how we look at the books that we see.

These are some of the reasons why I believe that discourse, incubator programmes and workshops are so important. In Mexico,

    *Ana Casas Broda*

for example, it is still very complicated to publish a photobook. If you get the interest of one of the few big publishers, the author usually cannot make many decisions, as designers have a long and important tradition and their work in books has a leading role. Nor has there been much possibility for choosing materials, since the usual papers are few and conventional. Experimentation with cheap and easily accessible papers of national use became key in Hydra's publications and is now a feature of some other publishers too. We began to print our editions on our inkjet and laser printers, binding them manually. This gave the books surprising and enriching qualities. We also do larger print runs in hybrid production schemes combining industrial and manual processes, to make it possible to publish books at a more affordable cost, not relying solely on the possibilities of commercial printers. For longer runs, this is expensive and it is a struggle to work with a printing industry that is unprepared and rarely willing to experiment, as most printers are geared for commercial printing on standard materials.

The mix of cultures in photobook education is an important start, something that is particularly enriching. It is only in spaces of real exchange that the core points of identity, culture and history of authors from different countries, continents and social strata are touched upon. Whilst it is essential that narratives delve into issues of local relevance and significance, their dialogue with other experiences, worldviews and ways of working is vital for a culture of resistance, not only at the local or national level, but in forming values that are shared in the creation and construction of narratives that generate meaningful dialogues and exchanges. The ways of working in different countries and continents are very diverse. Cultural, social and economic contexts inevitably generate possible forms of work, collaboration and production with their own themes. For this reason, it seems to me that a true criss-crossing of experiences and intercultural learning is fundamental. This means not copying external models, but developing a critical dialogue and collaboration that contemplates all phases of the creation and materialisation of photobooks in different parts of the world with specific contexts and issues. In this, educational processes are a key element that allows this critical reflection on the needs of the contemporary photobook and how we envisage change in this medium of so many possibilities: an agent of real change with a greater reach in society.

*The Photobook as Social Object:*
*Redefining Boundaries*
Anshika Varma

Anshika Varma is a photographer, curator and artist
from New Delhi, India. She is the Founder and Publisher
of Offset Projects, an artist initiative working with
photography and bookmaking.

I remember walking through the streets and by-lanes of Urdu Bazaar
in Old Delhi as a teenager. An endless lane of printing shops where the
rhythm of the calligrapher's hands found harmony with the pace of my
footsteps, watching sheaves of paper being cut, stitched, bound, and
piled up to deliver different stories for us to reside in. I could never
read or understand Urdu, but I respond to it instinctively, as a language
whose presence evoked a profound sense of belonging. This
experience allowed me to perceive language beyond the constraints
of script, engaging instead with its sonic and affective resonances. In
many ways, I hold the same relationship with photography: in its ability
to relate to the literal and the metaphorical simultaneously, I find the
photobook can free itself from constraints we sometimes believe
photography must remain bound to.

My engagement with publishing has deepened my understanding
of what made books so integral to my sense of self. Beyond being mere
objects of consumption, books function within an ecology that invites
participation – not an industry, but a community. The relationship
between the body and the book is central here: the book comes alive
when shared, both as a process and as an object. The iterative
expansion of photography over the past two decades has underscored
the urgencies behind a work, examining how the book-object offers
depth, rhythm, and narrative structure that resonates with its reader's
embodied experience. This act and its authoring have empowered many
practitioners to consider what their work can address, breaking the
structures of what the photobook has meant historically, allowing for
shifts in form and interdisciplinary approaches in storytelling.

With these stories placed in readers' hands, I feel publishing has
managed to stay true to photography. The photobook's evolving
materiality is evident in its ability to collapse linearity, generate
temporal ruptures, and create intimate, parallel worlds. Sanjiv Saith's
*Happy Goodnight* (2019) and Adil Hasan's *When Abba Was Ill* (2014)
exemplify this shift, situating the book as an existential entity that
resists traditional sequencing. Dayanita Singh's self-published books
*Zakir Hussain* (1986) and *Portrait of a House* (2021) have both been
reprinted and reimagined in expanded formats with Steidl's *Zakir
Hussain Maquette* (2019) and *Apartmento* (2025) respectively. Often
published under her imprint Spontaneous Books, her book objects
expand on her practice as an artist, prompting ideas of chance, time
and production. The artist's book, often confined to an internal
landscape, also becomes a site where the personal and the political

are deeply interlinked. Himali Singh Soin's lick-able stamp book *Static Range* (2022) considers the geo-political ramifications of the Nanga Parbat mountain in the Indian Himalayas providing a conceptual space for reflecting on nuclear culture, porosity, toxicity, and post-nationhood. Similarly, Prarthna Singh's *Har Shaam Shaheen Bagh* (2022), Rohit Saha's *1528* (2019), and Alana Hunt's *Cups of Nun Chai* (2020), mobilise the photobook as a vessel for counter-narratives, demonstrating how photographic storytelling can contest dominant historical accounts through extremely personal experiences, bringing new modalities of artistic practice to define the structures through which the photobook is created and disseminated in South Asia. The transformative potential of the photobook is further reinforced through its engagement with archives and embodied histories. Priyanka Chabbra's *Rock Paper Scissors* (2024) reconfigures an archival collection of documents encountered during the filming of *Pichla Varka* ('*The Other Side*'), layering historical and political narratives within domestic and gendered identities. By incorporating multilingual poetic responses and dramatised dialogues, the book situates the archive within the artist's own familial history of Partition displacement. We see the further manifestations of these inextricable connections in books such as Ishan Tankha's *Still Life* (2024), Soumya Sankar Bose's *Where the Birds Never Sing* (2020), Indu Antony's *Why Can't Bras Have Buttons?* (2021), and many more.

The urgency of photobook publishing as an act of resistance is evident in projects such as Gauri Gill's *1984* (2013), a downloadable photobook accompanied by a small print-run which documents the anti-Sikh pogroms in Delhi. Gill's project, updated iteratively from 2013 until 2021, reflects an expanded understanding of the photobook as a living archive – an evolving site of research and political intervention. This adaptability reflects the photobook's capacity to function as both a tangible and discursive entity, engaging in alternative economies of knowledge production. The scarcity of photography publishers and the absence of any state and cultural support for publishing photography in the region gave the impetus to a wave of self-publishing. A movement that came parallel to the decline of print media outlets and the presence of photographic voices in traditional editorial spaces, these acts cannot exist in isolation. They pass through an endless network of sharing knowledge, resources and finding unique formats in which the book finds its home. Artists such as Sohrab Hura have played a big role in making self-publishing seem accessible with his first book *Life is Elsewhere* (2015). Published under his own imprint UGLY DOG, Sohrab worked with local printers and textile shops for the production of his books and actively shared these resources with many photographers, helping them develop their works and taking them to the printers, encouraging them to make dummies and explore the possibilities of this medium. While we might see a proliferation of published material find recognition today, for each book that finds its imprint on an offset press there are multitudes that live as dummy books in the homes of artists as they find finances to bring them to life. The Alkazi Foundation Photobook Grant, initiated in 2016, has given support to the production of artist books, working in collaboration and offering financial support to produce books under the foundations publishing practice. It continues to be one of the only photobook grants in South Asia even today.

The act of world-building through the book form becomes an act of reclaiming power and rewriting histories. It offers us a chance to imagine new realities, challenging normative ways of working, creating spaces for new experiences and inviting us to reconsider possibilities of photography becoming a universal language. For the language to grow, we must let it find its echoes in multiple worlds: those that reside within photography, and more importantly, those that remain outside of it. Publications such as *DALIT: A Quest for Dignity* (2018), *The Public Life of Women – A Feminist Memory Project* (2023) from Nepal Picture Library and *Witness* (2017) from Yaarbal have been seminal in establishing and putting in place a range of photographic counter narratives, belonging to the people whose histories are being told, brought to the forefront. In a region where border tensions remain volatile, bookmaking has become a method for artists to redefine boundaries through collaborative exercises. Independent publications such as *Bridging the NAF* (2019) by Thuma and Kaali collective and *The Land of Pakistani Tress* (2018) by Farside Collective allow for the book to reflect upon conversations emerging from cross-border solidarities in the region. The artist book can be seen as a vessel for this transformation: a space where we can experiment with different truths, where meaning is fluid and multifaceted, where new rules can be imagined, and where reality itself can be questioned. It is where the reader, too, is invited to engage in the process of meaning-making.

I am keen to think about the relationship of photography with the larger world. Through a question that has remained at the core of our inquiry at Offset Projects – 'How can we work with the language of photography to help bring ideas and thoughts together… to converse, research and understand the world we occupy?' – I want to draw our attention to the relationship of the book with the reader as much as the author, as recipients of objects that assert their worlds in the physicality of our bodies and demand our submission into the ideas that create them. The library at Offset is called the Pitara, a trunk that contains innumerable readings and curations that travel from clean white rooms to the chaos of the streets, to festivals, schools, and community centres. We have sat in parks and asked people to come read with us. The architecture of this world contained a kaleidoscopic soul and every week, when we came back to set up our trunk, we found more people would gather: couples out for a walk, a writers' group, children out for a Sunday picnic, and those wandering through these gardens curious to find a group of people huddled together in silence. For that moment, these readers owned the stories that photography allowed us to see. It was humbling and freeing to know we had no control over what stories would exist in the hands of the reader. These interactions affirm the book's capacity to transcend authorship, allowing meaning to emerge through reader engagement.

During an iteration of the Pitara – at the Chennai Photo Biennale – I had placed a work by Sean Lee, a Singaporean photographer who adopted the persona of *Shauna* for many years and found himself at a point where he had to choose which of these two entities belonged to them. While he became Sean, a book emerged for Shauna who was an important part of this moment in his life. I remember observing a woman enter the reading room and sitting with this book for hours. In my conversation with her I found out her son that very morning had told her how he found himself trapped in the body of a boy. To clear her mind and think of ways in which she could address this, she decided to step out for a bit and found herself in this room with the book right in front of her. These are not just chance encounters. These are moments where the echoes of why we photograph reside. In this ever changing medium, photography has shown me that it remains open and welcomes transformation as its constant.

Our publishing ethos comes from the belief that the book is a ground for companionship, a shared room where we can experiment and work together to find formats for each artist's intentions in a work. Workshops such as The Photobook Intensive annual programme have been central in our exploration, and throughout the Asia-Pacific, initiatives such as Reminders Photography Stronghold in Japan,

Matca in Vietnam, Photo SouthAsia, Gueari Galeri in Indonesia, PhotoKathmandu in Nepal and Chennai Photo Biennale in India, among many more, hold regular workshops and residencies to develop a deeper understanding of the medium and support independent book practices. The growing recognition of photobooks within regional and global festivals such as The Singapore International Photo Festival, Focal Point in Sharjah, Hong Kong Photobook Festival, Kyotographie and KG+ Photobook Fair, many of whom also host dummy book awards to support the production of artist books, signals an expanding engagement with this form.

*Guftgu* (2020), our first publication, was created with a deep desire to think about how the voices of the artists could serve to initiate conversations on subjects presented by them. This core intention led us to question the form that certain books take when featuring multiple artists, something that I refer to as the ego of the book, where the format of the book begins to dictate how the works are presented. I wanted to celebrate each work and show the process and motivations of the artists' practice. I believe these internal deliberations for us and many practitioners in the bookmaking world are the true marker of a growing bookmaking community: it is not only about photographers making books but the coming together of people and the unknown exchange of ideas that emerges from it.

While printing Uma Bista's work, *Stay Home, Sisters* (2020), no matter how much ink we poured into the offset machine, the paper was unable to give us the deep reds we needed for her images. Exhausted and unsure of how we were going to make this happen, I sat with the printer and spoke to him about the work. I told him how the red, signifying a woman's menstrual cycle, reflected the artist's frustration at a practice that treated women as objects of a patriarchal system. The red was fire, it was anger, it was strength. It could not be anything but a deep fiery red. He heard me silently, told me to wait in a meeting room and said he wanted to try something. The proof that came after was different, more saturated. It was our final proof and is what exists in the book today. Later, once the book was printed, bound and packed, he came to tell me how that conversation stayed with him when he went home and spent time with his kids. It stays with me every time I open the book.

The references in this piece are by no means exhaustive, and offer a small glimpse into the multitude of movements around the photobook medium I have observed in recent history, shared in the hope that it might resonate with concerns and shifts in the larger contemporary visual practice. I imagine the book as the manifestation of a site that holds no firm ground: it is fluid and its space emerges from the pages that hold worlds contained in it, created by those that bring it together and specifically those that are birthed from its imaginations. In the folds of its paper is embedded the memory of our contemplations and urgencies. Moulding the book to locate the experience of world-building is central to the deep and intimate relationships that appear within our work and engagements. It is in the resonance of these encounters that I believe the book finds its belonging.

# Hans Gremmen

*Hans Gremmen is a graphic designer based in Amsterdam, The Netherlands. He works in the field of photography, architecture and fine art and has designed over 300 books. He has won various awards for his experimental designs, among them a Golden Medal in the Best Book Design from all over the World competition. In 2008, he founded Fw:Books, a publishing house with a focus on photography-related projects. Together with Roma Publications, he recently founded ENTER ENTER, a project space in the centre of Amsterdam which explores the boundaries of the book.*

*What were the encounters which started your relationship with photobooks?*

It began when some friends from art school from the photography department wanted to make a collective zine about their work. They asked me to be involved to work on that. I really liked their invitation, and because it was a zine, I also felt lots of freedom to come up with way too many ideas. Those zines evolved later into magazines, and after that into books. However, the feeling of freedom and experimentation continued through all the other publications. Equally, an idea that you work on with friends never changes. It is an ideal, because most of my collaborations start with mailing people who I haven't met before, but sometimes we end up working several years on a project, which creates an intense and special relationship. These collaborations can only exist when there is no hierarchy. We both have to keep an open mind for each other's ideas. This means both to move out of your comfort zone. That way, new things can happen and are created.

*How do you balance choices between working with highly specific materials or processes, and the desire for access?*

Perfection is fine conceptually, but it should never be the goal. In fact, I think perfect books are very boring. A book should have an edge, some friction. I mean that a book should have some level of desire to make you uncomfortable, because in that way a viewer has to bring something to the book. You are going to be sharper, more present when looking at the work. Perfection lets the viewer be lazy.

It is also not too complicated. Friction can occur when there is a blank page, or when there is an image of a tree in an edit full of portraits. It shakes the viewer, and keeps them on point. And this aspect makes you aware that we are making and looking at a book, not a machine. A book should follow some rules, but also shouldn't be afraid to break those rules too. For me, this is one of the most important aspects in editing. Further, a book is also made within the restrictions of an industry. If a quote from a printer is high, that is a signal for me that the puzzle is not yet solved. For me, this is an indication that the system of printing and binding is not working for me, but against me. I always try to use the system in the best ways possible. This often means that productions are economically healthy, and in general means a best use of paper, technique and production process.

I like to work within the limitations and restrictions the industry gives me, even if I like to question the restrictions from time to time. I also like to create within reasonable budgets to prevent the creation of expensive books. We aim for our books to be affordable and accessible for (art) students. When we were in art school ourselves, books were an important part of our inspiration and research. And Fw:Books also started as a group of students making books, so we feel very connected to that audience, and therefore making books accessible for them is always important.



The idea of borders, and – in a larger context – continents doesn't really exist in books, I think. We work with people from all over the world, with different views and backgrounds. There is always common ground. The other side of this story is that I think our books should be available for everybody. If you take something, you also have to give something.



Often people come to me saying: "I worked for years on this body of work and want to make a book to finalise the project". That is a wrong view on what a book is. A book is a beginning, not an end. Also, the relation between photography and books is very unique. There is no such thing as "original" photography. Photography is always a reproduction. Whether it is a C-print on the wall or printed in a book, both are as original. This perspective means a book is a work of art, not a random container of work. The only way for the photobook to survive is if it stops to exist as a genre.



We try to keep our print runs as precise as possible, and when in doubt, we keep it on the lower side. This saves on transport, paper, storage and other costs. It's a very small gesture, but the idea behind it is to try to be critical towards what we are making. However, it is always a dilemma, and a "catch 22" situation. For instance, we wrap our books in plastic. It's not that we like plastic, but if we don't do it, we get books back often because they are damaged. That would be creating extra shipping, handling and waste. It is always a matter of pros and cons. We have explored, for this specific issue, the use of biologically disposable plastics, but these are not yet good enough to seriously consider. I have hopes this will evolve in the very near future.

*What would make a better photobook ecosystem?*

If you mean the "photobook ecosystem" as "photobook world", then life is too short to think in boxes. Books can have texts, photography, drawings, clippings, art, theory, questions, answers, perspectives, microcosmos, expanding universes, confusion, fiction, facts. Books are books. The photobook should get out of its own self-imposed golden cage and join the other animals in the zoo!
    If you mean "photobook ecosystem" as an "ecosystem", in the environmental sense, I don't think it is my place to make general remarks or suggestions about this, because I think people should be able to make whatever they want, and however they want.

*Who have been the models or templates for your own activities?*

Second-hand bookstores. The great thing about these places is that you can browse through books, without a fixed plan. You have to take it as it comes. The books are sometimes organised by genre, but often not really. It is nice to just look at what you come across. Also, it is good to realise that books have a life after the first buyer. Every now and then, I come across a book I was involved in, and makes me very happy to see it there, not thrown away, but patiently waiting for the next person to pick it up, to enjoy it.

*What's currently on your desk?*

A never-ending "To-Do List".

    *Hans Gremmen*

# Valentina Abenavoli

Valentina Abenavoli is an editor, book designer and visual artist working at the intersection of photography, video, sound, and text. She has led intensive workshops on photo editing and bookmaking internationally. In 2012, she co-founded Akina, an independent publishing house producing challenging photobooks by emerging photographers. Her first photobook, Anaesthesia, was released in 2016, followed by her second book, The Harvest, in 2017. Both are part of an ongoing trilogy investigating the subjects of empathy and evil. Recently, she co-founded Neighbour, an alternative art space in Trivandrum, India, focusing on exhibitions, publishing and collaborations.

When it comes to books, there's neither a clear beginning nor an
end. It's an ongoing, evolving relationship. It wasn't a sudden spark
or love at first sight. Rather, it grew slowly, rooted in childhood, in
stories, in diaries filled to the margins, in old family albums like entire
encyclopaedias of strangers. Something deeper stirred within me,
drawing my mind toward far-off places and revealing the beauty in
life's most ordinary details – all recorded and preserved in printed
form. Books have always been the proof of lives lived. They offer a
suspended moment in time, a refuge from reality, an open invitation
to step into an extraordinary "other" world.

When I think of my life before working at Akina, I recall a
fascination for photobooks that was raw and unshaped – an early,
unrefined intuition that supported an imaginative approach without prior
knowledge, in its mad and vast simplicity. I would pick up a book
because of its cover or title, without knowing what to expect with each
turning page. As I learned the narrative structures and rhythm of
sequences, I took my sweet time with each book, and some stories, in
all their complexities, would linger in my mind for a long time, unfolding
in multiple serendipities and nocturnal epiphanies. It was a real pull, a
magnetic one, that had been the primary subject of my thoughts for
many years. That blissful ignorance is what I now miss deeply.

Many years ago, while still studying, I worked at a book fair in
Torino, Italy, in a rather simple role. I was responsible for handing
out microphones to writers and publishers as they took the stage.
In between talks, I would slip away to wander the stalls with Federico
Clavarino, who, years later, would become one of the artists Akina
collaborated with. Together, we flipped through the works of Italian
photographers like Letizia Battaglia, Luigi Ghirri and Mimmo Jodice.
At times, we kept an eye on the clock to avoid missing the next talk,
but then one of us would inevitably get lost in the spell of books –
the weight, the texture, the world of a stranger offered to you as the
most intimate shared space. These books were far too expensive for
me, so I filched a few. It's a good story to mark the beginning of my
relationship with photobooks. There was a desire to understand the
realm of these visual storytellers, using the book form to express
and communicate something invaluable – an expensive magic.

In the same city, around the same time, I would often spend

hours among the dust-coated wooden shelves of La Bussola, a local bookstore selling old, preloved and out-of-print titles. These books waited for someone – anyone – to come along and rescue them from the anonymity to which they were relegated. Sometimes, I think many survived years under the indifferent dust of the bookshop only to gather a new layer of dust on someone's shelf at home. The gesture of taking a forgotten, preloved book that could be reintroduced to someone's life, where it might one day be opened again, its pages turned by another's hands. There was a kind of timelessness to it, a quiet, slow resistance to finitude, defying the rules of a fast-paced market, where books need to be sold out within the same year of release. The photobook selection was scarce and mostly generic, but some obscure gems I still own today were found there, on a corner shelf labelled '*fotografia*'.

When this fascination for photobooks found me, beyond the coffee table books of famous photographers whose names I never learned, there was a growing urge for independence in photography – a push against the establishment, a need to create something outside the mainstream. From the underground up. I see now the sense of rebellion that led me to want to be part of that movement of zine makers and cheaply produced books filled with loud content and honest rawness. I started collaborating with a literary agency, learning editing, publishing and marketing. But I think it wasn't enough to simply work with books. I wanted to create the book object itself, from scratch: the design, the choice of size, paper, sequence, and text. A book is more than just a collection of images or words – it has the intrinsic quality of being made by many hands, collectively contributing to different stages of creation, production and dissemination. I wanted to be part of that effort to create vessels of beauty and change.

It is an everlasting joy and a never-ending pain, my relationship with photobooks. It has its roots in intuition and surely changed my life when it began, but I haven't yet figured out how much I've changed in relation to them. It used to be all I could talk about – books, books, books – and I still do, even though Akina no longer publishes, and I no longer stand on stages, advocating for space and support to experiment with new ways of expanding the market beyond its bubble. I'm just quieter and more specific about it now, which seems to go well with age.

*What is your process for arriving at decisions about
books and the projects that you undertake?*

As a publisher, I was once drawn to photographic projects that
required courage, often tackling controversial or thought-provoking
subjects. I was keen to engage with works that had the potential to
spark conversations, provoke complex social dialogue, or explore
political and existential themes. If the visual narrative was compelling
enough, I believed that words weren't necessary in the book. But both
the market and I have changed since then. What excites me most
today are projects that embrace interdisciplinary approaches, where
photography is one part of a larger composition – often working
alongside text, illustrations or video stills. In this context, the book
itself becomes a form that embodies connections between disparate
elements. Each spread follows the next, creating both linear and non-
linear relationships between subjects, objects, actions, places and
time. These parallel narratives, and the potential meanings they carry,
are familiar to us and can be part of a larger scope, like a symbiotic
root-like system of interconnections.

The concept of the "third image" created by the juxtaposition
of two images placed side-by-side is that inexplicable mental image
that words cannot express, yet it's something we all understand and
discuss when reading, teaching or analysing photobooks. Being by
contrast or by accumulation, this is a catalyst for endless possibilities
and effects. It reflects a state of being mutually dependent, not only in
the natural world but across different disciplines as well. It speaks to
the emotions we give and receive, the long-term use of knowledge,
and the process of unlearning in order to learn again. It really
highlights humanity's complex relationship with both the known and
the unknown. And in this sense, the more we look at the world in an
interrelated way, the more we can deepen our sensitivity to various
subjects and towards each other.

There is a clear need to bridge the gap between art practices
and academic research, as both fields can benefit from each other's
insights. We are too accustomed to thinking, working and acting within
the photography niche, but by doing so, we often tend to congratulate
each other's results without truly challenging the way photography
can serve as a carrier of meaning. If we are curious about humanity,
we would only benefit from collaboration, which allows us to better
contextualise knowledge beyond specific areas of study.

    *Valentina Abenavoli*

We often formulate projects based on our imagination and speculation, and I am deeply fascinated by this potential, by the process itself. I like to linger in the urgency of ideas that provoke thought with no immediate purpose other than offering alternative perspectives. I like the aftermath of creation, when the work becomes at the service of an audience to be dissected, interpreted, carried forward in any iteration possible.

Over the years, I've come to realise that a new model of the art world is needed, one that challenges the individualist culture of authorship and creative production. I prefer to engage in works that are rooted in collective experience and that are participatory. This is where my interest in collaborative authorship began – where books and exhibitions are the result of dialogues, negotiations and exchange, and where there's a certain acknowledgement of the new forms projects have taken, emerging from a shared creative responsibility of multiple voices. Artists, writers, designers, curators, and editors add layers of meaning, context and interpretation of the work, making it a complex and dynamic entity beyond the purely artistic expression. It is within this space of mutual influence, where roles and responsibilities intersect, where I find the greatest creative potential to break down the hierarchies in the art world and maybe create a more sustainable model for all.

I think moving to Kerala, India, and working primarily with artists and institutions from the Global South for the past five years, has given me a different perspective on what collective narratives can achieve. This shift from the individual to the collective requires rethinking agency itself, recognising that personal stories are always entangled with larger social, political and economic forces. It means moving beyond isolated experiences to examine the structures that shape them. There's a need to decolonise our understanding of stories and power, and I believe this will always shape my collaborations moving forward.

*How do you like to work with people?*

Meaningful conversations are the foundation of how I work with artists. I believe that truly listening to someone's story is essential in my role as both editor and designer. I like to be convinced, questioned and challenged. Serving the potential of the work, bringing forth everything that is yet to be said or seen. This requires not just a deep understanding but also a healthy mix of empathy, respect and imagination to translate these works into book form.

Trust is built by being open to each other's vulnerabilities. There was a time when conversations with artists were so visceral and emotional that hours would pass without eating or sleeping, leaving my mind on fire. I've only recently learned the importance of saying "no" and setting boundaries. I experienced complete burnout once, and it took me two years of healing and rest to be able to absorb what an artist wanted to share and to help them navigate the book form again.

Now, I'm much more selective about the projects I take on. Becoming a mother gave me a new perspective. The urgency I once felt to engage with every intriguing project has shifted. Now, I weigh not only the potential impact of a project but also how it aligns with my current priorities – mental health being one of them. There's still a bounce of ideas and shared vulnerabilities, but it's a slower, more considered process.

*How do you balance choices between working with highly specific materials or processes, and the desire for access?*

My practice began with a clear focus on balancing specific materials and processes with accessibility. In 2012, we at Akina started printing and binding handmade books at home, inspired by zine culture as a revolutionary, accessible way to spread ideas. Without funds for offset printing, we explored new approaches to both content and form, collaborating with emerging photographers. We managed to get trial machines twice, and published four zines and two books in editions of 100 to 200 copies each, paying only for the paper. London, at the time, was alive with creativity, and we had the support and courage to leave stable jobs for counterculture.

Over the years, we produced handmade books in two editions – a standard and a collectible edition – at prices people could afford (£8 to £12 for the standard edition, £35 to £50 for the collectible). All the books sold out within a very short time, leaving us often with a backlog of production and long nights spent surrounded by obscure vinyl records, managing humidity in perpetually damp London and stacks of paper covering every inch of our space.

The idea was to meet the needs of both collectors and those who wanted to be part of the community but couldn't usually afford expensive books. It was our way of addressing the divide we saw in the photobook market, where books either became collectible and expensive or were inaccessible to many artists and readers. It was also the proof that limitations – being money or materials – can really help creativity to strive, instead of containing it.

Large companies reach broader audiences with offset printing, lowering costs and benefiting from wide distribution while producing high-quality books. However, I never worked with distributors, and staying independent and sustainable was challenging. Eventually, we decided to shift to offset printing as demand grew, but in doing so, the books seemed to lose their intrinsic value of being unique. That was when it stopped being fun and transformed into something more rigid – a business governed by profitability frameworks. Although I partnered with a visionary printer in Istanbul, Ufuk Sahin, known for his ability to challenge the impossible, creativity can become subject to the pressure of meeting market demands. This leaves less room for failure when the investment is too high. I don't have the answers. Ultimately, I closed my publishing house after eight years and many books produced.



It's the tactile experience, the quiet moment of slowly unfolding someone else's work in a sentimental manner. In a world that's increasingly digital and ephemeral, the book is an anchor, a testament, an act of resistance. When one begins to notice how a book feels, and makes a ritual out of it – picking it up, running the fingers over the cover, that first crack of the spine, the smell of the ink on the paper, the whole experience of reading becomes an encounter with its own physicality. It slows you down, draws you into its pace, and invites you to stay for a while. The book becomes a place, almost, one that you inhabit for a time. And what a profound, enduring form of communication it becomes – tangible, intimate and moving – capable of being disseminated while resisting the passage of time.

*Anaesthesia,* the work I am most attached to, asked to be a book from the very beginning. It emerged from a profound personal struggle, fuelled by anger at the Western bias of empathy towards the Middle East – a bias that has perpetuated the dehumanisation of certain populations, shaping cultural narratives and influencing perceptions for decades. The choice to work on a book – densely black in its form – was the most visceral reaction to a world of violence and indifference. In exploring how reality is documented, shaped and presented to us, the book poses a fundamental question: if we've been overwhelmed by images of horror and war, becoming numb to the suffering of others, how will we choose to respond? Through the way the images and words are placed in the book, I wanted to invite others to feel, to pay attention, and to have radical positions towards humanity. Now, one year into the ongoing genocide in Palestine, on the verge of a much larger escalation, we are still bearing witness to our collective history, we are still challenging the false narratives. That book is a small testimony.

*What is the place of language and writing in a book of photographs?*

I've always loved the freedom that lingers at the edges of the image, outside of the frame. It is where the reader is really able to imagine. When words are offered, language becomes at once illuminating and restraining. The writing evokes what is not immediately visible. It guides, suggests, hints and eventually offers a way to begin, without ever telling you how to end. But also, words can impose. They can point to specific narratives, excluding, in part, the infinite possibilities of imagination. On the other hand, words that are not descriptive, and that generate abstract meanings, can create a beautiful tension, where text and image subvert each other's autonomy, pulling in opposite directions – one towards specificity, the other toward openness.

An intellectual controversy that has accompanied photography since the beginning is whether it can be defined as a form of language. I've often thought it is reductive to classify it this way, and I believe its unreliability as a form of language is one of the reasons why contemporary photography often relies on archetypal symbols, such as an isolated house in a bare landscape or hands holding something (or each other). These are simplistic, symbolic representations used to convey meanings of relationships, of belonging, of loss or identity, but they are not arranged in a systematic structure, which leaves them open to a certain simple interpretation without offering the precision of language. Many might disagree and argue that this approach opens up the ambiguity of photography for viewers who lack visual literacy. Words allow for precise and systematic communication, yet they also leave room for ambiguity due to the absence of a precise visual

    *Valentina Abenavoli*

representation. On the other hand, when images are overly symbolic, they offer a clear visual representation but lose the ambiguity inherent to the photographic medium. I am looking at that isolated house, and I cannot imagine another type of house, which, in itself, reduces the interpretative imagination.

I believe the only way to resolve this dilemma – and to elevate the photobook market to the same level of prominence as written books – is to make visual literacy a common subject, continuously and at every age, in every educational institution. To be more mindful about the current world as it is represented in images. Because art asks for a dual engagement: a visual one and an intellectual one. And too often it leaves out those less familiar with the other "language".

*Who have been the models or templates for your own activities?*

In many parts of my life, I can trace exactly where it all began – the contexts in which I gathered each facet of the person I've become, the moments when decisions were made, who stood by me, and who drifted away. It's like a vivid map made of memory lanes and sentimental journeys, and I cherish every turning point, each past version of myself. There is a series of consequential events, and connected people, that have led me here, now, in Trivandrum, with my partner Joe and our son Eli.

It was 2015 when I met Sohrab Hura in Arles for the first time. He is not only an incredibly talented and considerate artist but also a reliable friend who has this unique ability to connect like-minded people. With a short and precise email, he introduced me to the wonders of Nayantara Gurung Kakshapati, the founding director of photo.circle, Photo Kathmandu and Nepal Picture Library. It took a year and a half before I could finally meet her in Kathmandu, and we spent a full week in one of the most immersive and life-changing workshops I've ever run. I have pictures of the students editing at 4am, with book cover cloths wrapped around our heads like veils. After that week, we began calling each other "mama". I believe it was love from the start, but also the joy of finding that our complementary skills allowed us to create something powerful together.

Nayantara's work is about the transformative power of visual storytelling – not just as art but as a force for social change. Together, with a growing team who feel more like family to each other and to me, she's shown how photography and visual media can empower communities to reclaim their own stories. These aren't just acts of creativity, but acts of rebellion against dominant narratives. What makes their approach special is that it's about building systems that nurture relationships and spark long-lasting dialogue. It challenges the status quo, drawing from indigenous knowledge to reframe ideas of inclusivity and equity, using art, ecology and political stands as collective tools for change.

In 2018, during my artist residency for Photo Kathmandu, I stayed at a guesthouse in Durbar Square in Patan. Every morning, the temple bells would wake me at 5:30am, and from my window, I'd watch people of all ages and backgrounds interacting with the exhibition *The Public Life of Women*. It was surreal – people staring, reading, commenting on archival images of women who made history, all before dawn. It's unimaginable to have such public engagement in the West at that hour, let alone one that addresses themes of gender and society. It made me question who we create art for and why.

I find myself thinking often about the present – about what role I have in our community, and how deeply Nayantara and the photo. circle family have inspired me. My mind drifts to Neighbour, the space Joe and I are about to open here in Trivandrum. It feels like the necessary next step, an extension of everything I've learned and believed in as an artist, a publisher, a designer, an educator and as a witness to current times. Neighbour is the combination of books, art and coffee, basically what makes my everyday. It is a reflection of our hope to engage with the world through the act of gathering, of being present with one another. I hope we can become a catalyst for change – however small that might be at first in our neighbourhood – where conversations can have that imaginative narrative, and books and art can push boundaries, challenge perceptions and ask difficult questions.

# Miguel Del Castillo

Miguel Del Castillo is a writer, translator, editor and curator. He was born in Rio de Janeiro and lives in São Paulo, Brazil. Named one of the best young Brazilian novelists by Granta, he is the author of Restinga (Companhia das Letras, 2015) and Cancun (Companhia das Letras, 2019). He coordinates the Photography Library at Instituto Moreira Salles (IMS) in São Paulo and was formerly Editor at Cosac Naify and ZUM magazine's website. Del Castillo previously published an online column on photobooks and is now pursuing an MA in Literary Theory at the University of São Paulo.

I began my career at Cosac Naify, an art and literary publishing house, where I started as an intern before being hired as an Assistant Editor for children's books. After a few years, I also began assisting with architecture and art books, as well as handling image rights. Eventually, I had the opportunity to become a full editor, overseeing both architecture and photography books. I had the opportunity to work on books by notable Brazilian artists such as Bob Wolfenson, who, in *Belvedere* (2013), explored a series quite different from his renowned work in fashion, focusing instead on photographs of decaying tourist spaces. With Vicente de Mello, I collaborated on *Parallaxis* (2014), which brought together several of his series. Our aim was to create something that felt less like a catalogue and more like a photobook – a reflection of his life and artistic journey. I also worked on *Contrastes Simultâneos* (2014) by Walter Carvalho, whose photographs in the book closely echo his acclaimed work as a cinematographer.

At this stage, my studies in architecture, combined with my interest in photography and experience with art books, played a crucial role. Additionally, my work with children's books honed my sense of sequencing, and my ability to handle image-text relationships and page transitions which are vital in photobook editing. In fact, I believe photobook studies could benefit significantly from the theory and criticism that surrounds children's books. Following my experience in publishing, I was invited to join Instituto Moreira Salles (IMS), which was then developing a new museum in São Paulo. I was tasked with leading the Photography Library, building its collection from the ground up, and developing public programmes centred around photobooks.

To kick off the collection, we first established our priorities: the primary focus would be Brazilian photography, followed by Latin American, and then international works. Our aim was to gather as many photo-publications as possible from Brazil, while being more selective with foreign acquisitions. We already had some books that were purchased for curatorial research, as well as the Stefania Bril collection – around 1,000 books which demonstrate her important role as an articulator of the photographic circuit in the country, with an eye in tune with the international production of her time (the 1970s and

80s). From there, we formed institutional partnerships, established contacts with national publishers to acquire more books, and purchased several private collections from key Brazilian figures, giving us a solid foundation to build on.



I strive to think beyond a niche, especially when developing public programmes around photobooks. In São Paulo, there are many specific initiatives that are valid and interesting, but I aim to foster interest among a broader audience. At the IMS library, we have a dedicated space for photobook exhibitions, and I curate selections that appeal to the general public. For example, at our opening in 2017, I presented an exhibition titled *São Paulo in the Photographic Book: 1954–2017*, which aimed to highlight, through books, the city's inequalities and rapid, ongoing transformations. Subsequent displays have included a focus on books about military dictatorships in South America.

Previously, at the publishing house, I was fortunate to work closely with in-house graphic designers. This setup is somewhat rare, especially in Brazil, where the editorial team is typically fixed, and graphic work – like covers or the entire design – is usually outsourced to external collaborators. Having graphic designers integrated into the team from the very start of a project was a real advantage. We were able to discuss ideas from the initial concept phase, make adjustments throughout the process, and refine every detail all the way to the final product. This close and continuous collaboration between the designers and the editorial team was a powerful catalyst for the bookmaking process. The ability to brainstorm, revisit decisions and fine-tune both the visual and editorial elements together made the creative process much more dynamic and cohesive. It allowed for a seamless exchange of ideas, resulting in books that were more thoughtfully crafted from both an editorial and design perspective.



Being a non-librarian heading a library has significantly shaped how I approach this question. I greatly benefit from my team (including librarians), who offer valuable perspectives on book culture and knowledge sharing. First, what does it mean to create a library dedicated to photography, with photobooks at its core? For us, it means expanding a specific audience and democratising access to photobooks. We achieve this not only by having quality books available but also by fostering an open, welcoming space without membership cards or access restrictions – some visitors even come to work on their own projects. We provide direct access to shelves and promote talks, study groups, book exhibitions and thematic selections.

As editors, we may not always consider how to distribute our books through libraries. Early in the IMS library's journey, artist Rosângela Rennó gave a lecture in which she said something that has since become our guiding principle: "Photobooks are how we'll explain what photography was to future generations. We must fill libraries with them; they cannot be confined to private collections." When I talk to editors now, I try to convey this idea. It doesn't have to be our library, but it could be their local library or the museum library near their home. To condense this into one sentence: I believe the audience for photobooks is still quite limited, but libraries offer a powerful way to broaden it.

*How important is it for photobooks to reach other continents?*

I believe it's essential for the general public to have access to books from diverse places and cultures, as much as possible. At the IMS library, our priority is Brazilian books – we aim to collect everything published locally to preserve our photobook culture. However, we also include foreign books in our collection. When we started, we acquired private collections built between the 1980s and 2000s. Only later did we realise that most of the foreign books were from North America and Europe, as those were the main references and the ones available for purchase here. In response, we made a concerted effort to acquire more books from Latin American, African, and Asian authors for our archive. This required active research and engaging in discussions with scholars and researchers who specialised in these regions. We also had to recognise that, even today, many voices from outside North America and Europe are still being published by presses within these continents. Acquiring books published locally in places like Africa, for instance, remains a particular challenge due to issues such as limited distribution channels and prohibitive shipping costs. Navigating these barriers has been an ongoing effort, but it's essential for ensuring that our collection has the broadest representation of voices.

I can't speak directly for authors regarding how it impacts them when their books are recognised or showcased abroad, but personally, if I were to publish a photobook, I'd love to know that it was being seen in a library in Mexico, Japan or elsewhere in the world.

*What do you think is the significance of the shift towards the book as an object?*

There is something in this idea that started to bother me, especially while establishing the library at IMS and developing our access policies. While it is indeed important to recognise the photobook as a three-dimensional object with unique qualities, I've found that this perspective can sometimes lead to treating it as an untouchable work of art. At IMS, we decided to keep most of our books accessible on open shelves for the public to browse. Just because a book might cost $300 from an online reseller (due to multiple speculative reasons), it doesn't mean it should be kept away from users.

If one of the main ideas behind creating a photobook is to provide a more accessible experience than a traditional reproduction, then it doesn't make sense to publish it only to confine it under a glass dome, where people can see only the open spread or, at best, view a video of it. Of course, there are exceptions for older, more fragile books that require special handling or artist books produced as unique editions. But in general, I advocate against the unnecessary sanctification of photobooks. Books are meant to be touched, seen and flipped through; they should be accessible for people to engage with and share.

*What is the place of language and writing in a book of photographs?*

As a writer myself, I have a particular appreciation for books that balance writing and images, where both elements complement, provoke or even contradict each other. I'm not referring to photobooks that include a preface or postface (although those can be valuable), but rather to books where text and images are intertwined more deeply, such as *El infarto del alma* (1994) by Chilean photographer Paz Errázuriz and writer Diamela Eltit, or the Brazilian classic *Paranoia* (1963) by poet Roberto Piva and photographer/graphic designer Wesley Duke Lee. Contemporary examples also abound, with specific categories even created for this kind of work, such as in the Arles Book Awards.

Maureen Bisilliat, an English-Brazilian photographer, offers a compelling approach with her series of books that pair extracts from renowned Brazilian writers (like Guimarães Rosa, Jorge Amado and Adélia Prado) with her own photographs, creating new narratives she terms 'photographic equivalences'. She challenges the cliché that "a picture is worth a thousand words" by asserting that her photographs are only complete when paired with text. I once curated an exhibition about this aspect of Maureen's work, which I called *Writing with Images and Seeing with Words*, a quote of her own. This perspective adds a rich layer to the discussion of photo-text books.

I also believe there's much to learn from children's book theory in this context. For instance, Sophie van der Linden's *Lire l'album* (2006) notes that: 'In picture books, texts and images sometimes ignore each other, contradict each other… But they cannot be compartmentalised or separated completely. Present together in a single space, that of the double page, they are apprehended by the same gaze and necessarily relate to each other from a formal point of view. It is therefore a question of appreciating the occupation of space by these two languages, their own characteristics, their arrangements, the effects of resonance or contrast… Considering that, at the formal level alone, there are already countless implications in terms of narrative and discourse.'

*Who have been the models or templates for your own activities?*

Before the opening of our library in 2017, I extensively researched various art and photography libraries around the world for inspiration. The first ICP Library was definitely one of them. I was also particularly intrigued by Stiftung Sitterwerk's advanced system for digitally emulating book shelves, which uses a robotic scanner to recreate book spines side-by-side. Although such a system could be valuable for remote users, what I learned from their effort was the importance of allowing visitors to physically interact with shelves, and that's exactly how we decided to approach our own library policy. There's something uniquely rewarding about browsing freely and stumbling upon a book you weren't specifically looking for alongside one you were. We also drew from independent initiatives like TURMA in Argentina, which has developed a library and a space for courses and activities, as well as other Latin American institutions such as Mexico's Centro de la Imagen and Uruguay's Centro de la Fotografía (CdF), with whom we continue to stay in touch.

In terms of publishers, Steidl has been a key partner from the beginning. Gerhard Steidl's significant impact on photography publications since the 1990s is well recognised. He also decided to collaborate with us to host the first Steidl Library, which includes a complete set of his publications generously donated to us.

*What's currently on your desk?*

I have the privilege of working in a room adjacent to the library, which means that each time I go to the bathroom, I cross a long corridor lined with tall bookshelves filled with photobooks! This constant visual presence is quite stimulating.

Recently, I've had two Brazilian photobooks on my bedside table. One is *Sete Quedas* by Shirlene Linny and Júlio Cesar Cardoso (2020), an in-depth visual investigation into the story of a brutal kidnapping and murder of an ambassador during Brazil's military dictatorship. The other is *República das Bananas* (2021), a strange and brilliant fiction created by Shinji Nagabe. Additionally, I had been frequently revisiting *Entre* (1974) by Polish-Brazilian photographer Stefania Bril, as I have been working on her major exhibition, entitled *Stefania Bril: Desobediência pelo afeto* [Disobedience through Affection].

# Yumi Goto

Yumi Goto is an independent curator based in Japan, specialising in comprehensive production, curation, photo editing, publishing, research, consulting, education, and talent development in photography. Her work focuses on conflict, contemporary social issues, human rights violations, and women's issues. She has collaborated with humanitarian and human rights organisations on photography campaigns and publications, and has served as a judge, nominator, curator, and producer for international photography awards and festivals. Yumi is the co-founder and curator of Reminders Photography Stronghold (RPS), where she facilitates diverse activities related to photography. In 2020, she also established the RPS KYOTO PAPEROLES initiative and continues to be actively involved in its development.

*What were the encounters which started your relationship
with photobooks?*

In 2013, I had the opportunity to meet Jan Rosseel in the Netherlands,
and that encounter deepened my understanding of photobooks. His
artist's book *Belgian Autumn* (2015), which was his graduation project,
deals with a series of violent robberies that took place in Belgium
in the 1980s, by the so-called "The Gang of Nivelles". The book
weaves fiction and non-fiction, exploring the blurred and unreliable
nature of memory. Jan's work focuses on the intersection of historical
events and personal memories through visual storytelling, and it was
incredibly inspiring for me.

This meeting marked a turning point, where I came to see
photobooks as not merely containers for works, but as vehicles to
deepen and reconstruct the work itself. The next year, Jan and I
started a workshop called PHOTOBOOK AS OBJECT. It helps artists
better understand their own works, supporting them through iterative
processes of creation. As is evident in *Belgian Autumn*, the ways in
which themes and stories are embedded into the very structure of a
book has become a core focus of my photobook-making practice today.

*How do you like to work with people?*

When working with others, my priority is ensuring that the themes
we tackle can contribute to a better understanding of the world or
facilitate social change. Whether collaborating on projects through the
Reminders Photography Stronghold programmes or mentorships, I
aim to engage with work that provides new perspectives and insights
into the respective worlds of artists.

Through the creative process, I like to have a clear vision of the
final outcome whilst working closely with artists to help them achieve
their goals. However, the ideas generated by the artists themselves
are equally important. I believe in constant dialogue, continuously
checking in with their concepts and working through them to reach
the best possible outcome. Over time, I've observed that many of the
artists I work with struggle to maintain a clear image of the finished
product throughout the process. Therefore, my role often includes
facilitating their expression of a comprehensive vision while supporting
the step-by-step development of the work.

*How do you balance choices between working with highly specific materials or processes and the desire for making accessible books at mass productions?*

The artist's books we collaborate on are often what I call "signature works" for the authors. The limited edition is intentionally fixed to reflect the value of the work itself, which makes it difficult to reach a broad audience. That said, when considering the fundamental role of a book, I believe that wider dissemination is equally important. To achieve this, we ideally collaborate with partners who have the know-how regarding the production process. This way, the book transforms from a mere commodity into something far more meaningful.

It becomes possible to collaborate with publishers and editors when an artist's book has won awards like the Dummy Award, or when said work has enough influence within its community to be recognised. These works gain persuasive power, compelling publishers and editors to consider mass production.

*What is the public for a photobook? Who do you think of as your audience?*

I believe the public nature of a photobook is not just about reaching as many people as possible. It is about how its message speaks to society and creates dialogues. Photobooks are physical objects that carry ideas, emotions and historical contexts, and their significance lies in how they are presented in an accessible way to diverse audiences.

Though the artist's books I work on are often signature works with limited editions, if the messages they contain address important questions of our time, they shouldn't remain within niche communities. The public for a photobook isn't confined to art lovers or those within the arts community. It should reach broader audiences – readers with various cultural backgrounds or even those outside the arts – challenging their viewpoints.

In my work, I imagine my audience as those who seek out new perspectives, people who are curious about personal and social stories and those who reflect on their own lives and ideas through art. Many photobooks I've worked on hold the potential to transcend cultural and geographical boundaries and encourage cross-border dialogues. In this sense, a photobook's audience is as much about the people who encounter it as it is about the work itself as a platform for engaging with social conversations.

*How important is it for photobooks to reach other continents?*

It is incredibly important. Not only does this transport the work physically, but it also creates opportunities for dialogue across different cultures, histories and social contexts. A photobook is a unique medium that communicates through both visual and tactile experiences, allowing for deep connections with its audience. It transcends language barriers, delivering its message in ways that are visceral and universally felt.

When works travel across continents, they introduce diverse perspectives, sparking new understandings and inquiries amongst people with different values. I find this to be one of the most exciting aspects of photobooks. We operate within our social and cultural frameworks, but this medium can break those boundaries, encouraging empathy and recognition of differences.

For creatives – artists, designers, publishers and printers – reaching other continents opens doors to new markets and collaborative opportunities, fostering global exchanges and growth. For me, photobooks travelling across different borders isn't just about international exposure, but about creating meaningful dialogues with different communities and learning how the work is received within different contexts.

*What do you think is the significance of the shift towards the book as an object?*

I am not particularly interested in materials that are merely aesthetically pleasing. Instead, what matters to me is how a book is designed as a device that draws the viewer into the world of the work. I prioritise creating books that are not just objects, but immersive mechanisms – books in which every element is calculated to enhance the viewer's experience.

For me, books shouldn't only serve as physical objects, but also as mediums that allow an audience to dive deeply into the narrative or theme. How the tactile experience of turning the page, the texture of the paper, the elements of design and the type of binding relate to the story or concept is crucial. A book's intent and message should be conveyed not only visually but also through the physical and experiential aspects of its creation. Thus, the shift towards the book as an object is significant not for its aesthetic design but its role in deepening the dialogue between the work and the reader. It transforms the photobook from a mere collection of images into a fully immersive experience that draws the reader into its world.

*What is the place of language and writing in a book of photographs?*

In a photobook, I believe that the role of language and writing is to resonate with the images. Writing doesn't need to explain the work; sometimes, the most minimal use of text can still serve its purpose. When there are subjects involved, carefully constructed text can help ensure that there is no misunderstanding about their context or intent. Strong consideration of every word is vital when incorporating text into the photobook.

Additionally, writing that emerges from research and reflection, which offers us new insights or perspectives, is equally integral. In some cases, the artist's own research may take the form of an academic essay, included in the book to complement the photographs. It's essential that the writing is not simply recycled from existing literature but is something original that the artist has discovered through their deep engagement with the subject matter.

The most important aspect is that the writing and photographs interact to translate the artist's world or perspective in a way that is unique to them. The text should complement the images, whilst the images enhance the text, resulting in a more profound and layered experience for the reader.

*Who have been the models or templates for your own activities?*

As I mentioned earlier, Jan Rosseel has been a significant influence on my work. *Belgian Autumn* introduced me to the power of visual storytelling and the ways in which photobooks can reconstruct and express memory and history. He taught me that photographs are not merely records, but carriers of emotion, narrative and social enquiry. Through my collaborations with him, I learned the importance of not

just the final product but also the process of refining a work through
trial and error. His attention to photobooks as physical objects
that also serve as devices for communicating a creator's vision
had a profound impact on my approach to creating photobooks.
PHOTOBOOK AS OBJECT, now 10 years old, explores more than just
visual beauty, also emphasising how a work conveys its narrative and
immerses its audience. Over the years, many artists and participants
have joined us in exploring new possibilities for photobooks, and I
believe this workshop will continue to play a vital role in the field.

*What's currently on your desk?*

At this very moment, sitting on my desk is the trade edition of Kenji
Chiga's *HIJACK GENI* (2024), along with the artist's book and dummy
that led to the 90 limited edition copies. Together, these books
offer glimpses into the process of creation, showing the journey
from concept to form. I also recently acquired a beautiful book by a
completely unknown Kyoto art student, Aoto Tokui. Entitled *SHUFFLE
PLAY* (2024), it was made in an edition of only 50 copies. Small
discoveries and unexpected encounters like these are what keep my
creative spirit alive.
    Aside from the books, my desk is a blend of work and everyday
life, almost a kind of organised chaos. The computer screen displays
the manuscript of a new project, where ideas are taking shape. Next to
it is a worn-out calculator, a remnant of past work, and a small orange
plush toy, which is no mere desk ornament, but something that offers
moments of inspiration and serves as a creative companion. One
corner of the desk holds a pile of notes and receipts, but they have
accumulated naturally over time, not in disorder.
    This desk is where ideas and projects wait to become reality,
a small world where thought and creation intersect.

# Aneta Kowalczyk

Aneta Kowalczyk is a self-taught photo editor, book designer and art director at BLOW UP PRESS. The books she has designed have won several awards, including the European Design Award (2024), POY81 Pictures of the Year International (2024), Polish Graphic Design Awards (2019, 2022), Prix Bob Calle du livre d'artiste (2023), International Photography Awards (2018, 2019, 2020, 2021) and Maribor Photobook Award (2020). She also been shortlisted for Les Rencontres d'Arles Book Award (2022, 2024), Lucie Photo Book Award (2022) and PHotoESPAÑA (2018, 2019, 2020, 2023, 2024).

In my case, it was a natural development. Everything started with the
first publication we produced within BLOW UP PRESS. This was an
online monthly magazine dedicated to documentary photography,
*doc! photo magazine*. It was a real lesson for me as all my previous
design projects were related to corporate identity. Making the
magazine, being in a strict time regime, taught me to organise my
working system. It was something that was very useful when switching
to paper. From the beginning, we wanted our magazine to focus on
photographs, to let them talk, with as little distraction as possible.
We wanted to have all pictures visible in full, even if they were on
spreads, and we wanted the magazine to be a clear statement.
With all this in mind, I had to learn how to make it happen.

As I didn't like how some photo magazines were designed,
I followed the approach of the architecture and fashion magazines.
I cannot provide any titles here, but they all represented the highest
printing quality, and they paid a lot of attention to the images. They
were not afraid of big white spaces on the page, nor were they afraid
of placing the images on different parts of page and in different sizes
to let them breathe and give them a proper visual flow. And what is
also very important is that they used bindings and papers borrowed
from books, not from regular magazines. Much easier for me to list is
some photobooks or books containing photographs that inspired
me: *The Irreversible* (2013) by Maciek Nabrdalik, Karl Lagerfeld's book
about nothing but which is amazing as an object, *The Little Black
Jacket* (2012), and then two books by Japanese artists that are simply
masterpieces for me: *The Restoration Will* (2017) by Mayumi Suzuki
and *Silent Histories* (2015) by Kazuma Obara. And finally, *Parasomnia*
(2011) by Viviane Sassen. You can discover some of their solutions
and ideas in our magazine as well as in our books.

Seeing them, or experiencing them, I started to feel the need
to create something more durable than a magazine, something that
would stay a bit longer, a book. It was necessary for me to free myself
from the magazine routine or the magazine-like style of working.
I wanted to explore multi-layered and long-term projects, and to
create books that go beyond just presenting imagery and text. And
then, by the end of 2017, five years after the first issue of *doc! photo
magazine* was uploaded on our website, I designed my first photobook

– *9 Gates of No Return* (2017) by Agata Grzybowska, which became
a driving force for further books.

I'm still learning. It's not that you stop at one moment. If you do,
you risk that you will get into a routine and then all your projects will
look the same. For me, the most refreshing moment when thinking
about books and what they can look like, how they can be constructed
and from which materials, not necessarily papers, came when
visiting Ivorypress' collection of art books. If you happen to be
in Madrid, you should go there. This one visit may change a lot.

*What is your process for arriving at decisions about
books and the projects that you undertake?*

At BLOW UP PRESS, we have a motto which goes: "When the story
matters." And that is the most important factor for me when deciding
whether to undertake a project or not. I must feel the project, I must be
touched by the story. It must resonate with me and my emotions. Then
I try to understand the artist's intentions, motivations and thinking. It
takes a lot of time to enter into somebody's mind, but it is necessary
to understand all aspects of the project to transfer its complexity into
a book. And I definitely like to be challenged. I don't have any specific
topic I am looking for. I prefer multilayered, long-term projects; really
going into the details, exploring the story in all possible ways, where I
can see that the artist dedicated themself to making it.

The rest is a journey meandering through the project. All my
decisions are dictated by the story, whether we are talking about the
paper, book format, length, or layout. The book must mirror the project
and not simply insert it into some readymade graphic template. The
design should somehow be invisible, not to be more important than
the story it provides. Each decision taken by the designer must be
based on the project and how to make it sound its best, so that the
final reader will be impacted, or hopefully floored, by it.

*How important is it for photobooks to reach other
continents?*

Photobooks use the most communicative language of the world:
images. Thanks to this, they can be easily understood in any place in
the world. Therefore, reaching other continents should be something
natural. The bigger audience of the book, the better it is for the story,

its reach. Not to mention the artist, publisher and designer, of course. Imagine you live in Australia. It's a big country but contrary to its size, the photobook market is relatively small. So, if you want your story to reach as many readers as possible, if you want your project to be a game changer, you must go beyond some limitations, including geographical ones. It was also the case for BLOW UP PRESS. We come from Poland which has a population of 40 million people, with a visual culture that is in an early stage in the direct aftermath of Communist time and a lack of proper visual education at schools. If we were to count on our domestic market only, we would have been out of business years ago. As a result, we stopped making separate Polish language editions of our books as we would just lose the money on them. Besides, the English language is becoming more and more popular in Poland, so we reach our audience here anyway.



At BLOW UP PRESS, we often say we do not make photobooks but art objects. For us, each book is another galaxy with all its own secrets, dark and bright sides. Today, when you visit any photobook fair or bookstore, you will see many books coming from different publishers and artists that look exactly the same, created with the same templates I already mentioned. For me, the photobook's visual qualities summon experience and emotions and it is exactly this what I'm trying to reflect in my projects.

When I think about the book as an object, the only word that comes to my mind is experience. The reader should experience the book the same way the artist experienced the project. The role of the designer is to transform the artist's feelings into material form. And this materiality refers to everything, from the papers, through to printing techniques, the interactivity of the book in terms of inserts or any hidden content, up to the final book format and cover.

Let me illustrate this with an example. Recently, BLOW UP PRESS released the book *Eternal U* (2023) by Hubert Humka that covers the topic of passing, the life and death cycle, eternality. It consists of photographs of British forests existing as natural burial places. The artist came to me saying: "I don't want to have just a nice book with photographs of forest, I want an artbook. Do whatever you want with my photographs." It would be very easy to destroy such a fragile project using shiny coated paper or having a traditional approach to layout. In order to translate the artist's ideas into the final book, I decided to use recycled papers only, to emboss the entire text instead of printing it, and to create negatives from some of the photographs to reflect the cycle of life and death. I wanted readers to be lost in the forest, and so all photographs are printed full bleed. Thanks to embossing, the readers can also experience the bark of a tree if they touch the back side of the page. All this matters for this project and for this book. And all of this makes this book an object to experience. When a friend showed this book to his students, he told them: "Watch with your hands." So, as you can see, it is something more than just seeing and contemplating images. You must also feel them, physically. This makes the book a desired object to come back to, to collect, to think about in terms of the story it provides and to experience. Yes, it will cost more than a regular photobook, but it is worth making the additional effort.

*What is the place of language and writing in a book of photographs?*

They say that good pictures will defend themselves and in most cases it's true. But sometimes it is necessary to give them proper context so they can be read in the way the artist intends them to be seen, regardless of the place and the time. There are many examples of images that were misunderstood when they first emerged, or which outraged the public, and today we admire them. And vice versa. If we give them proper context made through writing, we feel more secure that they will be read in the way were made. Times change, our understanding the world changes as well, so does the reception of images. The same refers to photobooks which consist or may consist of such images.

Language in the photobook is also important. It's the same as with your question about reaching other continents. The more popular, universal or globally known the language you use in the book, the better for the book. As I said, at BLOW UP PRESS, we publish books in English as it is the most widely learned second language in the world, but in some books, we also introduce other languages especially when the project has significant meaning for the local community and/or the artist. What really matters here is to make sure that the text within the book does not overtake the meaning of

     *Aneta Kowalczyk*

photographs. We should remember that in photobooks, the story is presented through images, not through the text. The text here is always supplementary to the images. Not the other way around.

*Who have been the models or templates for your own activities?*

I am a self-taught photo editor and designer. So everything I know, I have learned from my own mistakes and obstinacy! However, there are two artists I would like to mention. The first is the designer Ania Nałęcka-Milach, it's thanks to her that I fell in love with photobooks. I am always impressed by her projects and how open she is to share her expertise with other designers. The second person is the amazing Yumi Goto. It's incredible how she can lead artists and their projects from the idea to the final object. They don't know this, but these two women shaped me as a conscious photobook designer.

*What would make a better photobook ecosystem?*

There is a lot that could be done to make it better. Proper visual education in schools and better state support for photobook publishers and sellers for starters. Also, a greater assertiveness among publishers to not be afraid to refuse publications when they see that the project is weak. Not all projects merit the book format, let's be honest. Some projects work much better in shorter form and others should never leave the drawer of the artist. We should all be more aware and conscious of qualities and the need for particular projects to provide readers with good books. They deserve this and we owe it to them.

*What's currently on your desk?*

A few projects such as the book by Polish artist Weronika Gęsicka titled *Encyclopædia* (2024). In it, manipulated stock photographs and AI generated images illustrate false entries she tracked down in different dictionaries, lexicons and encyclopaedias. Weronika comments on a contemporary world attacked by fake news that threatens the credibility of media and our freedom. It is another project that adheres to the ethos of BLOW UP PRESS, as fake news is now one of the biggest tools used to manipulate our opinions and minds.

It is a very important topic and working on this has been a privilege for me as through this book I can also mark my position on the phenomenon of information disorder.

# Raymond Meeks

Raymond Meeks lives and works in the Hudson Valley, New York, US. His work is represented in numerous private and public collections. He is the sixth laureate of Immersion, a French-American photography commission sponsored by Fondation d'entreprise Hermès. Exhibitions from this commission took place at the International Center of Photography, New York, US, in 2023, and Fondation Henri Cartier-Bresson, Paris, France, in 2024. The Inhabitants, a book made in collaboration with writer George Weld, was published by MACK in 2023.

I'd begun thinking about the book form when my children were very
young and my wife and I were building a small children's book
collection to read and share with my son and daughter. I was drawn to
certain illustrators, like Chris van Allsburg and Lisbeth Zwerger, where
a tale was heightened by provocative illustrations that contained
a balance of description and ambiguity to provoke the imagination,
to create suspension and leave room for the viewer's mind to add
dimension to a story. During this time, I was mostly working on
advertising commissions and photo essays for magazines… raising a
family. But I was also creatively challenged by assembling magazine
stories to accompany the writing. The combined interests dovetailed
wonderfully and sent me down the eventual path of bookmaking,
considering relationships between certain types of images, how
pictures activate one another to generate energy and feeling.

My bookmaking practice early on was centred around an
immediacy of making. This often meant trips to the hardware store
for materials such as tape, adhesives, paint, finishing sprays et cetera,
and developing an idea for what I might want the book to look and
feel like. In order to visualise this, I would visit one of a few used
bookstores in Missoula, Montana, near the small town where I was
living at the time, identifying an existing book that reflected and,
perhaps, informed one possibility for a book. I would deconstruct
and repurpose this book, working within the prescribed confines
of the former object, merging my printed pages and pictures with the
pre-existing form. These used books bore the influence of a past and,
by way of a quantum tethering, provided clues for the book I would
eventually construct. Direction could come from the title, graphic
design, existing story, page count et cetera. I liked to work intuitively
and without concern for accidents or mistakes, as either of these
allowed for the possibility of recovery.

I began shifting from considering pictures in terms of their
independent potential at a time when I was still heavily under the
influence of the "Decisive Moment", where each picture felt singularly
complete. There were very few books that were attempting to
construct in the serial manner that John Gossage envisioned with
*The Pond* (1985), where an experience could be constructed within
a contained world and was built from one page to the next, leaving

space along the way for the viewer to enter and participate. I wasn't aware of *The Pond* until many years after its initial release. I think, as a book, it was well ahead of its time and a break from the more traditional monograph, so the impact it had for me was quite profound. I don't have anything to add here – it's a nice balance of the personal, the process and the context in which you started to think about books.

*How do you like to work with people?*

I like to work with friends who already exist in my orbit and share some engagement in a creative process, inviting them into the fold of a collaborative project we can undertake together. There's something surprising and gratifying in encountering signs of their contribution, suggestions and choices made; a gifted title, an inclusion of text. This said, I tend to keep the work close and not overshare or invite too much feedback, less the edit/sequence begin to feel diluted or focus-grouped. Whilst I'm in the midst of creating and compiling pictures, there's a charged momentum and building of energy that I'm very protective of. When I've been more open to sharing in the past, I've noticed the energy and momentum begin to leak, like the releasing of a valve. I'm very careful about where I solicit feedback and try to do so only when I feel mostly resolved and understand whose insights would be especially informative and helpful.

As far back as I can recall, I've found it overwhelming to take in all the possibilities for a work of art, especially a book. Deciding that I'll only make use of whatever enters my field of play, be it materials, equipment, a subject or a collaborator, has served as a tremendous relief. What at first might feel like a limitation whilst working within these constraints usually opens up as an expansive opportunity, assigning importance to encounters that might otherwise feel random, cultivating a practice of paying attention, listening, developing and nurturing curiosity.

I also believe a finished work has the potential to feel more inclusive, accessible and relevant to a larger community whilst considering the influence of those in my trusted circle. That I'm attracting, whether actively or passively, the people and the elements that will contribute towards a final expression of a book or exhibition.

I tend to consider fellow artists (including writers and musicians)
as my audience, for better or worse. There are a handful of artists, in
particular, that I like to imagine encountering a book I'm in the process
of making, and then try to envision the ways in which the book speaks
to them or where it fails to resonate and for what reasons. If the book
succeeds, if it evokes feeling for these fellow artists, then I think it will
have the capacity to connect with a broader audience on a level that
regards their time, intelligence and imagination. Considering these
fellow artists as my audience presents a high-water mark, one that
invites risk-taking and reaching beyond my comforts or, perhaps,
a level I've previously achieved. I value our shared book form
tremendously, not just as an object, but as a communicative and
relational piece that participates in a larger cultural dialogue.

I've gone through periods of lamenting the notion of
photographers making books that mostly appeal to other book
artists. But then I realise it's no different for poets and their small
audience of 10% of readers, the majority of these being fellow poets.
Why should it be any different whilst charged with refining a visual
language that defies verbal description, forming active relationships
and sequences of images that generate ineffable feeling. We love
what we love.



I think the reception to a book is built into, and emerges organically
within, the process. I personally don't take responsibility for wanting
to make a book that spans continents, nor would I assign importance
to this. I think of a quote I read by Kiki Smith, where she says: 'Just do
your work. And if the world needs your work, it will come and get you.
And if it doesn't, do your work anyway. You can have fantasies about
having control over the world, but I know I can barely control my
kitchen sink. That is the grace I am given. Because when one can
control things, one is limited to one's own vision.' Not all books can
span cultures, nor should they necessarily aspire to. A photobook
can have immense value without a global audience if it serves a
deeply personal, local or culturally specific purpose, grounded in

particular histories, communities or aesthetics that make them uniquely powerful in a localised context. On a more personal note, I can make one distinction between artists that work along a horizontal plane and those that I perceive as working the vertical. The vertical plane drills down, narrowing with each rotation. For me, I centre on the personal – an obsession or curiosity, a question – even whilst aspiring for a connection with a broader audience. To the extent I'm willing to take risks and expose myself, to become vulnerable, moment by moment, with evolving clarity and detail, there exists the possibility that the evolving experience will explore and reflect a more common, shared state.



By attempting to make compelling books that have the potential to contribute to the evolution of the medium, to move the book's viability and existence in a bookstore to other sections in addition to Art & Photography. I think of applying my practice of bookmaking to "how-to" books or those that combine image and text in a less traditional manner. And with each book project, to ask, amongst other questions, what does this book want to become? The imperative in this question, for me, is: how can I approach my curiosity and deliver a book or form with some level of relevance to the current vibe, be it global or local – whilst not overtly addressing the political? How to shape an experience that will, hopefully, begin to reconcile chaos or conflict into an organised form of beauty, however fleeting? More generally, I suppose the lingering concern is what can I offer of singular significance. How can I be of "use"?



I suppose this would depend on the book of photographs. I personally don't apply rules regarding writing/text with photobooks, except that the writing avoids an effort to clarify the images or to limit their reading, thus eliminating the most meaningful role for the reader – to complete the work. I prefer when writing offers subtle direction without closing down around content or subject, or resolves points of indeterminateness. It's interesting when writing becomes an alternative to a picture, performing in a similar manner and in serial form. For example, early on in the collaboration with friend and writer George Weld on *The Inhabitants* (2023), I made a decision to refrain from making portraits of asylum seekers. This shifted how I began interacting with the landscape of northern France, the places of migration and provisional settlements. When choosing to photograph, I was drawn to composing around a conjured presence of refugees, partially summoned by my imagination, partially drawing from clues within the setting. The intent was to allow space for George to summon a voice for the displaced, bringing nuanced complexity and representing the immutable plight of the refugee. George's vignettes created a voice of displacement with the potential to activate the reader's imagination to construct a portrait. His portrayals, born of a year of research and fostering compassion, are more potent and expansive than what I might've made with a camera.

*Who have been the models or templates for your own activities?*

The artist James Castle, who found inspiration in the detritus of everyday life, primarily in the materials he collected from his family's home outside of Boise, Idaho, such as envelopes, packaging, advertisements, and matchbooks. Working mostly with soot, spit and homemade tools, he created a rich, complex style that was informed by the constraints he was born into. Castle was born deaf with limited means of communication. I recall first seeing his small books fashioned out of found materials and recognising how the immediacy of making was paramount and the transformative ways in which material instructs form.

*What would make a better photobook ecosystem?*

I like to imagine a system where small companies or maybe fashion houses would find value in aligning with a publisher, sponsoring the printing and distribution costs, allowing proceeds from book sales to funnel back to the publisher and the artists, encouraging the commitment to the book form. This system might also allow artists and publishers to take greater risks and empower a wider diversity of voices and makers, as well as contributing to the evolution of the book form.

# Luis Juárez

Luis Juárez is an editor, curator and cultural
practitioner in the field of photography, based in Buenos
Aires, Argentina. He manages artistic projects and
produces books, magazines, exhibitions, and art fairs.
He is the Editor and Director of Balam, the first and
only queer magazine dedicated to contemporary photography
in Latin America, and the Founder and Director of MIGRA,
Buenos Aires Art Book Fair. Juárez is a member of Archivo
de la Memoria Trans Argentina (Argentina Trans Memory
Archive), a space for the protection, construction and
vindication of the trans memory, where he coordinates
its publishing house.

The first time I had an idea of what it meant to create a publication was when I was 10 years old, in 2001. I was in fifth grade at my elementary school in Tegucigalpa, Honduras. My teacher assigned us the task of creating our own magazine. The magazine I made was about entertainment and music. I remember going to the print shop with my older sister. We stood in front of the place, surrounded by printing machines and stacks of paper, and I had to make decisions about how I wanted my magazine to look. Imagine the kinds of decisions a 10-year-old could make... The man at the print shop asked me what type of paper I wanted to use, what format I preferred, and how I wanted the magazine assembled. I remembered my sister telling me that she really liked my project. That moment marked my first, albeit unconscious, encounter with the role of editor and creator of printed matter. From then on, I developed a special interest and sensitivity for working with images and tangible objects.

Many years later, now living in Buenos Aires, Argentina, in 2018, I managed to print the first physical edition of *Balam,* Issue N5. Its theme was 'Metamorphosis', where we explored how images inherently carry a drive towards change. We created a document that brought together images and reflected on their productive process, and the desire to represent transformation. In the issue, we included critical and aesthetic contributions that helped us envision a new habitat, a renewed space where differences became metaphors that generated meaning. We proposed a break from normativity, offering alternatives to conventional forms. Or at least, that's what we aimed to convey. *Metamorphosis* was an experimental issue. My training as an editor has always been self-taught, and in this issue, I envisioned *Balam* for the first time as an object, more akin to the concept of a photobook than a traditional magazine. Although I call it a magazine, I appropriate the term to reimagine and understand what it means to work collectively.

The project began digitally in 2015, using the resources I had at the time: a computer and a desire to connect with photography. As a migrant without a single penny in my pocket, I later found a way to express myself through photography and paper. Migration, the lack of representation and the desire to create a space of connection outside the established norm were the excuses I needed to start making photobooks.

In my case, directing a project that is printed once a year means working periodically. Each issue of *Balam* focuses on a specific theme, chosen through a deliberate and reflective process. The decisions about content are guided by a central goal: to speak relentlessly about the realities of sexual minorities and dissident communities. This focus is not accidental; since its first edition, *Balam* was born out of an urgent need to provoke, question and give visibility to voices that have been historically silenced or rendered invisible.

The world of photography – especially where the greatest capital and decision-making power are concentrated – has long been dominated by dynamics that privilege academic and intellectual white perspectives. This bias perpetuates exclusions and hierarchies that leave many on the margins. For me, understanding these structures is not only important but essential, as it allows me to offer a conscious and active response to the established order. I use photography as an excuse, a medium to debate, confront and question the realities of my community. Beyond its aesthetic value, the images in *Balam* are tools for initiating conversations, challenging narratives and exploring new possibilities for representation.

The books I produce are not just objects, but spaces for collective reflection. I am particularly interested in questioning who has access to photography and the production of photobooks. Who gets to tell stories through this medium? What economic, social or cultural barriers limit access? These questions guide my practice and reinforce my conviction that working in community is the only way that makes sense to me. The decisions that shape my projects emerge from collective processes. I interpret and materialise these decisions, acting as a bridge between the needs expressed and the creation of an editorial object that engages with those demands.

I often reflect on the disconnection between academia and the realities of communities. I believe sometimes academia lacks the "streets" in its epistemology. It is easy to analyse and theorise from the comfort of a desk, but going out into the world, putting your body on the line and experiencing the tensions of social realities is a completely different practice. I firmly believe that this connection to the ground, to living stories, is what gives meaning and depth to my work.

In *Balam*, themes are not only decided but also discovered in the midst of the creative process. By deeply immersing ourselves in the theme of the current issue, we uncover ideas and connections that organically lead us to the next edition. This makes the project something alive, constantly evolving. I like to imagine *Balam* symbolically as a necklace: each previous issue awakens and nurtures what the next one will become. For example, Issue N8: *Chosen Families* awakened Issue N9: *New Masculinities*, and so on... This continuity ensures not only coherence but also a constant evolution in the discussions and reflections we propose.

*How do you like to work with people?*

For every issue, I collaborate with a guest editor. Together, we decide how we want to project and tell the story, from its concept to its materiality and design. This approach allows *Balam* to reinvent itself from scratch. Nothing about *Balam* is linear, because there is nothing straight. Each editor brings their own unique universe, inviting me into their world and challenging me to be even more politically incorrect. This process reaffirms that there is no single answer when it comes to creating and producing.

I'm not interested in working with "editors" in the traditional sense of the word. Instead, I collaborate with individuals whose connection to the proposed theme is deeply rooted in their way of life and personal experience. Their wisdom comes from lived experiences and emotional insight. This is crucial to me: learning from them, amplifying their capabilities and offering them a space to discover new possibilities within themselves. This exchange is mutual and deeply reciprocal. Without reciprocity, I'm not interested in collaborating; I cannot move forward.

As such, the selection of guest editors is never random. I choose to work with people I deeply admire and respect. These collaborations enrich me both personally and professionally, reinforcing my belief that creativity thrives in encounters and dialogues. By allowing each editor to bring their vision, the project becomes a platform for constant exploration. This methodology ensures that every issue is a unique and authentic exercise, where differences are not only celebrated but also become the driving force behind the creative process.

I would like to rephrase the question and reflect on "Who are the
people doing photobooks?". Instead of "What is the public for a
photobook?", who has access to the resources needed to make them?
Access to information and production tools must be universal,
regardless of the format. Only then can we truly work with
perspectives that are more real, inclusive and representative.

It's important to acknowledge that, historically, photography has
been a tool of colonisation, used to document and illustrate what
which was stolen from us. For example, in hundreds of photobooks
created by white men, we find the story of colonisation in the
Americas told from an external perspective, often stripped of context
and the voices of its true protagonists. Now, imagine what happens
when these books are printed and distributed across the world.
In the past, we had no choice but to rely on these narratives to learn
about "our history". There is a canon of European and American
photography that focuses on that, on celebrating the fetishisation
of our territory.

Today, the dynamics have shifted, and we have a responsibility
to challenge these narratives and actively work to bring photobooks
closer to their rightful protagonists. It is time to stop telling stories that
don't belong to us and to cease appropriating others' narratives. In my
case, my interest in creating books and magazines is deeply rooted in
working with the people who live and embody these stories. It's about
creating a safe space where they can tell their own experiences, from
their own perspectives, and see themselves represented in the
materials we produce.

This leads us to a crucial question: what does it really mean to
create a photobook? Do we want our book to simply be a product
that reflects our personal interests, celebrates the excellence of its
materiality and design, wins awards and participates in prestigious
festivals? Or do we want it to be a vehicle for amplifying voices, a
means to provide resources to communities and projects that have
long awaited the opportunity to be heard and seen?

If we choose the latter, we are engaging in an act of reparation
and social justice – a way to contribute to greater integration and
representation. This brings us to the pivotal question: are we truly
creating new narratives in photobooks, or are we perpetuating the

same structures of exclusion and centralisation of power? In my
case, before thinking about who my audience is or who the people
consuming my books are, I focus more on the audience I want to work
with. That is, I prioritise understanding the internal aspects over the
external ones. When the focus is on the internal, the external result –
the book as a final object – becomes a genuine reflection of the
relationships, learning experiences and conversations that took
place during its creation. The external audience is simply a natural
consequence of the final work. My attention is on the process –
on how and with whom I work with.

*How important is it for photobooks to reach other
continents?*

A photobook is much more than a physical object; it is the
crystallisation of ideas, experiences, narratives, and collaborations.
Reaching new corners in other continents is essential for these stories
to be understood, read and appreciated from different perspectives.
I work with the idea that books should be free of borders – a tool to
democratise other realities and expand the conversation beyond their
places of origin. At *Balam*, for example, we translate our magazine into
English, Spanish and Portuguese to connect with broader and more
diverse audiences. This not only allows our stories to reach more
people but also creates a space to find commonalities, shared
interests and representations across cultures.

This effort of distribution and openness significantly expands our
network, fostering collaborations with institutions, curators, artists,
and photography professionals from other countries. Reaching other
continents is not just an opportunity for expansion; for me, it is a way
to affirm and consolidate the ideals and methods I wish to work with.
It gives me a perspective on how things are made and thought.

However, producing the book is not enough; circulation and
distribution are equally important processes that require attention
and planning. Books don't move on their own. It is essential to build
relationships and experiences with the people and places that make
it possible to participate in fairs, festivals and other cultural events.
Especially if you're living in Latin America, where access to this
industry is hard to be supported. So going abroad is essentially to
position yourself and make new connections. In terms of financing,
for us historically, the money and the funding support is abroad.

In my case, after printing *Balam* for the first time, I was faced with the need to figure out how to move this independent project into new spaces. That's when I created MIGRA, Buenos Aires Art Book Fair. This project was not only a response to my own concerns but also a platform to connect with other projects and art book fairs around the world, like the Printed Matter Art Book Fair in New York, SPRINT in Milan, Athens Art Book, Recreo in Valencia and many others. Generating alliances and collaborations that strengthen the independent publishing community.

This work doesn't happen in isolation. It's an ecosystem where every element – creating the book, distributing and showcasing it – is essential for the whole process to function. Without one, the others wouldn't exist. And within this ecosystem, we're not just sharing an object but a worldview – open to dialogue and transformation.

*What do you think is the significance of the shift towards the book as an object?*

The shift towards the book as an object represents a profound evolution in how we perceive, create and interact with publications. It transforms the book from being solely a vessel of content into a multidimensional artefact – one that embodies not only the narrative it carries but also its materiality, as well as design and tactile qualities. Treating the book as an object disrupts traditional publishing paradigms. It challenges the notion that books are merely functional or consumable, positioning them on a different scale from conventionalism. This shift often aligns with experimental and independent publishing practices, where we as creators have the freedom to reimagine whatever suits our projects best.

Creating, editing, printing, and ultimately having a book read is, in itself, a performative act – a psycho-magic ritual that the photobook enacts. Each reader establishes a unique relationship with the book and its imagery, and for some, this connection becomes almost sacred.

When we print a photobook, we are working with the visual, engaging directly with what captures the eye first. This is where the emotional resonance of the work takes hold, forging an immediate, visceral connection between the viewer and the content. This process embeds the book with a profound affective dimension, making it inseparable from the individual who engages with it. Once this bond is formed, there's no turning back; the book becomes part of the person, a reflection of their experience and perception.

Photobooks, as tangible objects, carry a symbolic weight that contributes significantly to our construction of identity. We create and surround ourselves with objects that resonate with us on a deeper level, shaping and reflecting who we are. A photobook, then, is more than just a collection of images or stories; it is a vessel of meaning, charged with the emotions, ideas and identities of both its creator and audience.

This is why photobooks are often cherished as personal artefacts, not just artistic creations. They occupy a unique space between the visual and the tangible, where their physicality enhances their narrative power. The act of holding a photobook, turning its pages, and immersing oneself in its images and textures transforms it into an intimate experience. It is not just a book; it is an extension of human expression, a dialogue between the creator, the object and the reader.

*How do you attempt to address sustainability in publishing?*

The question of how to approach sustainability in publishing is complex for me. I work with and produce books independently in a context where printing is becoming increasingly difficult. This is due to several factors, one of the main ones being the economic crisis in Argentina. Additionally, there is a lack of cultural support and a shortage of collaborative projects that contribute to strengthening the photobook community.

In Argentina, *Balam* is the only contemporary photography magazine currently published, and one of the few in Latin America. Over time, I have noticed that printing costs continue to rise, which increases the price of the magazine for the market. This forces me to constantly think about strategies and partnerships to keep the project afloat. In fact, one of the biggest challenges is that many projects, due to economic reasons, end up becoming obsolete and disappear.

Next year, *Balam* will turn 10, something I never imagined would happen, and it remains relevant and alive. This leads me to reflect on the concept of sustainability, which in my case is highly influenced by the context. It is not the same to edit and produce a photobook in Switzerland as it is in Argentina, as the resources, opportunities, materials and access are completely different.

I believe that an established publishing house or an institution might be able to address sustainability and answer this question better than me. In my case, it is much more complex, as I am uncertain about how I will be able to print the next issue of *Balam*. Sustainability in my practice is linked to constant uncertainty.

It is important to consider that, for those of us working independently, sustainability not only refers to the ability to maintain a project long-term but also to resilience in the face of an economic and social environment that makes cultural production difficult. Sustainability in publishing, for me, also involves building connections, strengthening networks of collaboration and supporting the creation of spaces that foster diversity and inclusion in the publishing industry.

*What would make a better photobook ecosystem?*

To go outside of it, to move beyond its own limits. It is essential to engage in dialogue with spaces, people and institutions outside of what is established. Working with the concept of decentralisation allows for the opening of other worlds and perspectives, creating new possibilities for creation and reflection. Agents who can play an active role in institutions, reviewing and questioning key aspects of the history of photography. I believe that photography gains greater meaning when one steps outside of it. It makes even more sense knowing that this is our medium of work.

# Daniel Boetker-Smith

Daniel Boetker-Smith is the Director of the Centre for
Contemporary Photography (CCP), Melbourne, Australia, and
a curator, educator, writer, publisher, and photographer.
He is the Founder of the Asia-Pacific Photobook
Archive and regularly speaks at festivals and symposia
internationally on the subject of photobooks, photographic
publishing and self-publishing in the Asia-Pacific area.
Boetker-Smith has previously taught and guest lectured
for nearly 20 years at universities and institutions in
Australia, Germany, Netherlands, Malaysia, Singapore, and
the UK and US.

*What were the encounters which started your relationship with photobooks?*

In my last year of high school, I had a photography teacher who was a bit of a loose cannon pedagogically speaking, and also fancied himself as a jazz aficionado. He had shelves stuffed full of photography books in his office – classics by Walker Evans and Robert Frank, but also obscure Japanese photobooks he'd collected on his travels. I don't recall ever having any formal classes, but just remember looking at photobooks for hours. The teacher would smoke his pipe and play a Charles Mingus cassette tape loudly over and over again whilst I ransacked his shelves. He would shout over the music about structure, rhythm, tempo, and pattern in images and music, though I couldn't understand most of what he was saying I trace my 30-year photobook obsession back to those days.

The second important encounter happened over a decade later, in 2001, when W.G. Sebald's book *Austerltiz* was released. I was in my final year at university, and I had already read Sebald's *Rings of Saturn* (1995) a couple of years earlier. I had been enthralled by Sebald's weaving of interconnected stories and meandering reflections that placed me in the middle of his experiences rather than just as a "reader". I had read *Rings of Saturn* when I had been travelling in Australia and had been on a personal quest to meet my father for the first time. So, for obvious reasons, I felt a strong connection to Sebald's interspersing of photographs and text as a way of dealing with the past, memories and their fragmentary and non-linear nature. I became magnetically drawn to books that used digression as a mode of storytelling. Sebald created a space for me to embrace disjointedness as a valid way to construct and explore narrative, and to see the world. Since then I have sought out photobooks that utilise such strategies in order to present their tales. I enjoy their disruptiveness, poetic and anarchic quality, and essentially that is all I ever write about.

At this time, around 2001, I was looking at photobooks like *Droit de Regards* (originally published in 1985 in French, and later in English) by Belgian photographer Marie-Françoise Plissart, the seminal *In Flagrante* by Chris Killip (1988) and Rinko Kawauchi's two books published by Little More, titled *Hanabi* and *Utatane* (both 2001). It seems now, on reflection, that 2001 was a perfect storm in which a tsunami of elements from literature and photobooks coalesced in front of me in the very moment in which I was ready to absorb them. These photobooks all seemed to apply (in visual form) the very concepts I had found enthralling in Sebald – an ability to resist and deviate from a traditional model of storytelling; to eschew neat, teleological narratives. These publications cemented my obsession with photobooks, formed the basis of my MA thesis that I completed the following year and represented the starting point of my photobook collection/obsession.



I find it hard to categorise what I do, and therefore how I work with people is difficult to explain. I have published books but don't consider myself a publisher; I have helped hundreds of people with their photographic projects and their books but don't consider myself an editor or designer; I have curated exhibitions large and small but don't consider myself a curator; I have taught photography and art for 20 years but don't consider myself a teacher; and I often write about photography but don't consider myself a writer.

I still actually think of myself as a photographer, though I rarely make photographs anymore. I think I unconsciously approach everything I do *as* a photographer – one who also writes, publishes, curates, and teaches. So, to dig into that and return to the question, I would suppose that this base informs how I work with people. I come at any collaboration I do with a photographer with a sense of being "one of them", not as someone who sits in a position of power as the Dean of a College, a Gallery Director or publisher.

This background is evident when I'm working with photographers, mostly students or in workshops and masterclasses. It's very easy for me to pick out the images that are working – to identify the photographs that are benefiting or progressing the broader narrative or theme, and the ones that aren't good enough. It's simply a case, for me, of getting a sense of the background, the intent and the aspirations of the photographer (and the images) and then putting myself in the position of the photographer, as if it were my own project, to make decisions about the direction I think it needs to go, and how best it could be manifested as a book or exhibition.

One of the key elements of making an edit of a book is retaining a physicality to the process – printing out all the images, at all different sizes, sticking them in books or on the wall, printing and

     *Daniel Boetker-Smith*

binding a dummy, and sitting with these various incarnations always leads to good decisions. The other important element is spending time with the photographer in my library of books. At the early stages of thinking about a book, there's nothing more useful than sitting in a room of thousands of photobooks. This process starts with aimless looking, random conversations and is then followed by frenzied trains of connected thought, which leads to refinement, inspiration, clarity, and purpose for the book yet to be made.

I get the most enjoyment out of working with emerging photographers. After 20 years of teaching, I never became tired or lost the passion for looking at new work. Inevitably, most of my teaching focused around photobooks, and I always found collaborating with students on making their photobooks thoroughly enjoyable. Now, as Director of the Centre for Contemporary Photography (CCP), I get the chance to work in a more informal way with emerging photographers, without my teacher's hat on. I am constantly reaching out to people to ask them to show me their work. Spending time talking through an emerging photographer's work in-depth, and discussing how they can improve and move forward and getting excited about how it could look in book or exhibition form is a perfect day for me.



As most of my interactions with photobooks is as a collector, a writer and an educator, I would like to approach this question differently. I think the audience is the one with the responsibility, and here I am referring specifically to US and European audiences. Given that the focus of the photobook ecosystem in North America and Europe, it is easy for those audiences to be complacent, and only engage with the books that are placed "in front of them". One only needs to look at the 'Best of' booklists in *PhotoEye* or *LensCulture* or *The Guardian* etc., it is essentially a closed circle. There is an urgent need to turn the attention to Asia, to Africa and to South America. Some European publishers and collectors are already doing this to a small degree, however having a small number of gatekeepers isn't enough. The photobook world needs to recognise and reflect on its biases and inclinations. The best photobooks of the next 25 years will not come from Europe or North America, they will come from places like

Indonesia, Nigeria and Brazil. And they will come from photographers who have vital and important stories to tell.

For someone publishing a book in 2025, the best way to think about photobooks is that the audience is entirely different for each book, and that you have to almost start from zero each time. An audience can't be conceived of until the final book is done and in your hands. Make a book as best you can within your budget, and as close to what you imagined at the start – as close to the idea of the book that got you excited enough about to want to make a book in the first place. Then once the book is done, and you understand what it is you've made, start thinking laterally about who the audience could be. For your first photobook, trying to make something with a preconceived audience in mind is a recipe for disaster.

Part of my work here in Australia over the past 15 years has been to build a community of photobook makers and to work with others to grow the audience of those who buy photobooks. When I became the Dean at Photography Studies College in Melbourne, I made sure that photobooks were a central part of the curriculum for both BA and MA students. Now, the students that I taught 10–15 years ago are themselves teaching, so inevitably the "bug" has spread. Most colleges in Australia now have some sort of photobook course. I also ran (with Heidi Romano) the Photobook Melbourne festival in 2015, and have been involved with organising and curating major photobook events at festivals and in national art institutions like the Museum of Contemporary Art in Sydney and the National Gallery of Victoria in Melbourne.

I have also on many occasions ran events large and small with Justine Ellis and Dan Rule from Perimeter Books, Australia's unofficial epicentre of photobook publishing. Perimeter produce up to 15 books per year, distribute a long list of international publishers to book shops all over Australia and New Zealand, attend fairs across the world and regularly organise photo and art book events, launches and fairs. Their passion and friendship have been a big influence for me over the last decade, and they have built up a massive community here through their commitment and energy.

In 2021, I co-curated a major exhibition here at the Museum of Australian Photography, and it featured a number of internationally recognised "photobook" names, including Mathieu Asselin, Broomberg & Chanarin, Cristina De Middel, Laura El-Tantawy, Yoshikatsu Fujii, Gauri Gill and Rajesh Vangad, Zhang Kechun, Dana

Lixenberg, Max Pinckers and Alec Soth, alongside Australian photographers Ashley Gilbertson, Raphaela Rosella and James Tylor. Though this exhibition wasn't about photobooks per se, it was, for me, an added bonus to create a platform to introduce an Australian audience to some of the most important international photobooks of the past decade or so.

*How important is it for photobooks to reach other continents?*

Of course, it's vital to the future of the photobook that we push for and embrace diversity and access. I would again rephrase the question however, given that this book of conversations and responses will, I imagine, have a predominance of European readers. I would instead ask how important is it for *you* (the reader) to seek out books from other continents? I would say that it is your absolute responsibility.

European photobooks, though publishers will admit times are tough, at least have a readymade market on their doorstep, with a glut of festivals, galleries and fairs, and geographic accessibility. The issue for photobook makers and publishers from the Asia-Pacific region (and the same is true for South America and Africa) is getting their books in front of a European or American audience, where most of the buying happens, where most of the "hype" is, via competitions, awards and prizes. A small European bookshop, for example, will not survive through charitable gestures supporting smaller publishers located in Manila or Taipei or Auckland. A healthy and profitable bookshop needs to stock books by photographers who people already know; as a result most of the bookshops in Europe sell the same or similar titles. Therefore, it is the audience that needs to educate themselves about photographers, photobooks and publishers from other regions.

The opportunity to address this is threefold. At fairs and festivals, prior to their visit, audiences should research which publishers are present from other continents and support them if they can by buying a book. The cost of freighting books across the globe means the margins for these publishers are tiny. The more they can offload and not cart back home, the better. Another way for photobook buyers and collectors to assist is to use the internet smarter, follow smaller independent publishers, festivals and fairs in other countries, and be aware of newly released books that way.

The final way is, when traveling, to find and approach the local photobook shops, events and networks, and see who is doing what. Often, if you seek people out and meet with them, they will point you in the right direction to get a sense of what's happening in photography in that country. These three things mean more exposure for lesser-known publishers and photographers, and eventually this can lead to a more sustainable market internationally for those from Asia-Pacific, South America and Africa.

I try to do my part through my writing, in that whenever I am asked to feature or review new photobooks by a European or American magazine or website, I will only ever write about photographers and photobooks from the Asia-Pacific region. Drawing attention to these photobooks on an international platform might not translate directly to sales, but the hope is that a reader takes note and is made aware of other things happening elsewhere in the world, and uses this information to start to explore further.

*How do you attempt to address sustainability in publishing?*

I am not sure the sector can talk about sustainability in a cohesive way, as it's so different in each country. In our little corner of the world, we do what we can, but, in the broader scheme, we are at the whim of larger, cut-throat industries and costs controlling import, export, paper, printing, freight, and taxes that are all connected to the larger global economy and currencies. Most publishers print overseas (in Asia and Europe), making it pretty difficult to claim any sort of "green" practices.

Paper is no longer made in Australia at all (the last mill closed in 2023) so we have a huge logging industry that produces material that gets sent overseas, and then all the paper for book printing needs to be imported back into the country. This convoluted process is incredibly expensive, making it practically impossible to produce offset printed photobooks here at any reasonable price. The reality is that printing books in conservative edition sizes, ensuring that there is a market for each book, and working in collaboration with other publishers and distributors is the best that can be done currently.

*What is the place of language and writing in a book of photographs?*

I am firm believer that photobooks and literature are interconnected. As I mentioned, in response to the first question, my obsession with photobooks came from a kind-of literary realisation. Over years of teaching, I have often tried to make it clear to students that literature can be a source of inspiration and ideas for photographers, and that the best writers can provide road signs for how to think differently about how we deal with visual narratives.

Because of this, I often see and look for literary influences in photobooks, not just in their subject matter, but in the way they are constructed or use storytelling devices. I think photographers can learn so much from literature, not just classics by Virginia Woolf, Marcel Proust or Sebald, but more recently Rachel Cusk, Maria Stepanova and Karl Ove Knausgård, as well as others who tell stories in a way that connect with images, and can perhaps inspire photographers to take risks with their storytelling.

I would recommend all photographers be playful and experiment with text and writing. It doesn't necessarily need to end up in their photobook, and maybe no one else ever sees it, but the routine and the frustration and the pain of writing down what you are thinking is an immensely valuable one. I have learnt so much about photography from writing. It's the only way I am able to clarify my responses to images.

*Who have been the models or templates for your own activities?*

My activities regarding photobooks have developed organically and simply out of a love and passion for the medium. My starting point for a more professional and community-oriented engagement with photobooks was when I established the Asia-Pacific Photobook Archive in 2013. I had been back in Australia for three years and was decidedly frustrated at the focus on European and American photography and photobooks that I found here. I was so much more interested to see what was happening in this region. Having visited a few photography festivals in Asia, I had seen first-hand the energy and talent evident in the work being presented. From this came the desire to grow and push the awareness of the photographic community in this part of the world, and to nurture young talent. I wanted to play my part.

The idea for the Asia-Pacific Photobook Archive came out
of seeing the brilliant work that Larissa Leclair was doing in the
US (Indie Photobook Library) and Bruno Ceschel was doing in UK
(Self Publish, Be Happy), and wanting to take it one step further,
not just by collecting books but actively and physically sharing
them with new audiences. Different to the Indie Photobook Library
or Self Publish, Be Happy, the Archive was never intended to be
static. The goal from the outset was to get the books seen by
audiences in different locations, so I was very clear in our manifesto
that any books submitted to the Archive would travel to festivals
around Asia and the world. With this promise, in 2013 I started
attending more festivals and events, taking submissions and buying
books. I would take a suitcase or two of books from the Archive, and
set up a space provided by the festival to show these books. It was
a condition from the start that we didn't sell books, as the Archive
was never set up as a "business". Often photographers at these
festivals (in India, Japan, Indonesia, Malaysia, Singapore, and more)
were not in a position to donate a copy of their book to the Archive,
so I would buy it instead. The Archive is probably 60% donated books
and 40% books purchased by me.

At the start in 2013, there were very few photography festivals
and absolutely no photobook related events in the Asia Pacific
region. Chobi Mela and Angkor were the only two main festivals, and
didn't have a photobook element at this stage. But this soon began
to change, and now there are photography festivals in most countries
in Asia, and most have a photobook fair included. Alongside this,
there are many collectives and spaces for photography communities
to come together to share and support each other across the
Asia-Pacific region. As I said, Isabella Capezio (who runs the Archive
with me) and I attended festivals all over Asia between 2013–18, we
would curate a display of books that were simply for browsing, and
we provided photographer contact information for people to then
go buy the books directly from the artists. We attended events in
different places in Asia, and early on we were also invited to manage
the photobook activities of a few festivals in the region, running
reviews, bookmaking workshops, talks, and so on.

As the reputation of the Archive grew we started doing pop-up
events of Asia-Pacific photobooks even more broadly, in the UK (at
The Photographers' Gallery Bookshop), and at photography festivals
in Europe (Latvia, Dublin and Landskrona), and all over the US. The

books that people submitted certainly clocked up a lot of miles.

As time passed a lot more festivals had emerged across the Asia-Pacific region, and a lot of these events started running their own photobook fairs and developing their own collections and libraries, so the need for the Archive to actively travel became reduced, and the number of submissions we were getting also dropped off. Just before Covid-19, I stopped needing to collaborate with festivals and fairs as most of them now had their own photobook events and spaces to house their own collections. The Archive served its purpose at the time, and I am happy that we played a small part in the early days of turning the focus on to photobooks in this part of the world.

From the beginning we had a physical space for the Archive in Melbourne that was open to the public and managed by volunteers. This was a very important part of the jigsaw in the early days. Not only were the books travelling all over the world, they also were on display here in Melbourne. The Archive still has a public-facing space, is still open and we still have photographers, student groups and international visitors accessing the Archive, doing research and looking for inspiration. It's still a free and accessible resource.



I would like to think that in the coming decade the attention of the photobook and photography world will move away from North America and Europe and will recentre itself in other places – in Asia, South America and Africa. As I previously started to discuss, the photobook network in the Asia-Pacific region has developed over the last 15 years, and today there are dozens of events of all sizes across a range of countries. It has become a positive space, though not without challenges and limitations. With the rise in art fairs, photobook fairs and photography festivals in the Asia-Pacific region, European publishers are becoming more aware of the wealth of talent here. There are, each year, more and more books being published featuring non-European and non-American photographers. The difficulty and challenges for the ecosystem is at the ground level and is simple economics; this is where people like Jessica Lim (Angkor Photo Festival), Shahidul Alam (Chobi Mela), Gwen Lee (Singapore International Photography Festival), Anshika Varma (Offset Projects) and other even smaller organisations and collectives in other countries come in and are doing amazing work. These sort of initiatives and organisations need the support of the broader international photobook world. This is true also for South America and Africa. There are smaller groups, collectives and organisations that need the support of their European and North American counterparts.

With what is happening politically, it's pretty clear the world global economy is going to struggle in the coming years, so I do fear for book sales, especially for smaller publishers who work with tight margins, and with emerging artists without an established following. I firmly believe North American and European audiences need to keep pushing themselves to look outside of the photographers and publishers in their own countries. There are such rich and amazing stories being told in all parts of the world, and they need to be sought out beyond the shelves of their local book shop or book fair.

I find it a conundrum that the connectivity of the art world and the photobook community seems to keep expanding and improving, while at the same time, our political leaders and the majority of our voting populations become more insular and xenophobic. It feels like photography and photobooks, and the diversity of stories they tell, will become even more vital in coming years.

# Andrea Josch

*Andrea Josch is Director of the Art School at Diego Portales University, Santiago, Chile, Editor-in-Chief of* Sueño de la Razón, *a South American photography magazine, and member of the SudFotográfica Foundation, which, amongst other projects, made the research and publication of* Una revisión al fotolibro chileno (2019). *She previously edited the academic journal* Diagrama *and directed the Investigación-Creación de la Imagen MA at Universidad Finis Terrae, Providencia, Chile. In the last 25, years she has dedicated her work to university and informal teaching, participating in colloquiums and biennials in Latin America, in addition to carrying out various publishing projects.*

I studied photography in the early 1990s, at a time when access to publications was very restricted. I personally did not know many of the publications that had been made throughout the 20th century in our country and the region, and there was no research on photobooks. What did exist was a tyranny of glossy paper and a saturation of coffee table books that focused on generating patriotic discourses, as well as presenting (as they continue to do) the Chilean landscape in a pristine and proper way for tourism without delving into any of the social, political and cultural complexities that marked the reality of the country that was entering a transition process after the civil-military dictatorship.

In 1998, together with several photographer friends, we decided to found the collective La Nave. This was a decisive step that allowed us to explore the artistic practice of photography, as well as the idea of thinking about the problems of images. Shortly after, with César Scotti, we created OjoZurdo, a web platform dedicated to Chilean photography that also functioned as a small publishing house. Although the publishing project is no longer active, the love that César has always had for publications was essential in shaping my foray into the world of books, awakening in me the need to know more.

My interest in photobooks was consolidated by participating in three editions of the Latin American Photography Forum, organised by the Itaú Cultural Institute of São Paulo, Brazil. These meetings mobilised the idea of investigating and exploring both the networks in the region and the world of the photobook in Latin America, a process that culminated in the publication of *The Latin American Photobook* (2011), edited by Horacio Fernández. Furthermore, in 2009, together with Luis Weinstein and with the support of Roxana Moyano, Director of the Simón Patiño Center in Santa Cruz, Bolivia, we founded the South American photography magazine *Sueño de la Razón.* This project has been fundamental to my development, enabling me, over the years, to participate in critical thinking and the production of publications in collaboration with a diverse group of editors from all over South America.

*Sueño de la Razón* has allowed us to learn to connect with different perspectives on photography, opening a space for dialogue where we intertwine historical archives, visual narratives, contemporary practices, and critical thinking. In that same spirit, together with Horacio and Luis, we invited five other artists, researchers and a group of people from different disciplines to review and collaborate on a project that led to the publication of *Una revisión al fotolibro chileno*. These types of projects have shown me that book production in Latin America is a deeply collaborative and vital process to expand the narratives of our territories.



Editorial and curatorial work is, for me, a collaborative task. Both in my role as an editor and as an academic, I see company and companionship as a key process for creation. Every project I undertake is an exercise in active listening and feedback with those involved. Creative processes do not follow a linear path or a rigid methodology. Very often, I also dream: of diagrams, of narrative sequences, of material solutions that then guide the direction of the projects.

It is essential to create an environment in which all voices involved can feel heard and respected. The result of a project is never the fruit of a single mind, but rather of a joint process of discovery and exploration. This is what makes editorial and curatorial projects so rewarding, that they become spaces for mutual learning and co-creation.



I enjoy teamwork. The best ideas, in my experience, arise from deep conversations, from moments of sharing a meal, from having the time necessary to learn about the sensitivities and desires of others. The creative process requires patience and openness to understand what you really want to share.

Over the years, I have learned that working with my intuition and with people I resonate with on a deep level has been the key to achieving a meaningful result. I love when people open their files and memories, matters and mentalities. This enriches the artistic process, since the unique methodologies of each person are really essential to opening questions that invite critical reflection and the material experimentation that will then reach unexpected audiences.

To give an example, a little more than 10 years ago, I met Marcelo Montecino in person. I knew who he was before, I knew part of his relevant work and a little about his life, since he was linked to the Association of Independent Photographers (AFI), which was a group that emerged to take care of and protect themselves in the streets during the Chilean dictatorship. But one day, Marcelo wrote on Facebook that he was looking for information about a designer in Chile who knew about photography books. I suggested people, after which he told me that he was coming to Chile (he still lived in the US then) and asked if we could get together to talk about a book he was editing about women, since he knew that I was an editor. I couldn't be more excited, meeting someone you respect and admire for their work. From then on, our conversations, now in person since he has returned to Chile, transformed into a beautiful relationship of collaboration through his archive, his life and photography. The last book we published, *What a long and strange journey* (2019), brings together photographs belonging to his long stay in the US that he had never shown, along with a booklet where he comments in first person about life, the pain of political violence, the struggles of social movements, the loneliness of the elderly, trips across the country, and what photography is for him. It is one of the books I have edited that excites me and that I like the most, but I think that it could only be the way it is because of the collaboration, because of the regular lunches for some months with him and his life partner Lucy every Tuesday and talks about their lives in the north. This way of working, which is also a way of life and understanding, I believe enhances the capacity of artistic creation to resonate beyond a strict artistic field. It touches intimate fibers, the social and the cultural in a unique way.

*How important is it for photobooks to reach other continents?*

The journey of a book is in itself significant. It is part of its reason for existing, if it is understood as a desired opportunity to discover new perspectives and generate encounters with others. Of course, trips can involve crossing streets, neighbourhoods, regions or oceans. However, I do not think it is essential that they circulate outside their local contexts. I consider it more important to think, in advance, about what you want to communicate, to whom the work is directed and for what purpose it was carried out.

For this reason, I don't know if I agree with the way this question is worded, since it leads me to think about the fashion in which the photobook has fallen in recent years, seen as an object of desire, collection or investment. It has been losing the initial meaning of what it initially wanted to investigate, narrate, relate. I think of artistic and editorial practices as ecosystems that nourish our way of inhabiting the world, of opening questions, of thinking about presents and possible futures. Having said this, if the books manage to be read in other continents, it is part of their beauty, travelling to unexpected places to share diverse perspectives. This is a process that depends on how the publications end up spreading in remote places, by those who find them and pass them on.

The essential thing about the act of publishing is the commitment and responsibility of artists, designers, editors, distributors et al with the investigations, enquiries and/or political, poetic, intimate, cultural, social, ecological knowledges of the ideas that we circulate. This does not mean, in any case, that books or artistic works do not need to be appreciated and read by others, but rather something else, even opposite: we should start thinking that it is essential not to catalogue everything again as universalisable, since there will always be a diversity of readings that depend on cultural, socioeconomic, political, and familial factors. The singular universal occidental history has done us a lot of harm, placing to one side, for centuries, the multiplicity of stories that interweave and cohabit the world. Therefore, the relevance of circulation on other continents should be thought of with an ethical and critical stance, aware of how we want to circulate our own way of looking at the world.



I am not entirely convinced that there has been a change in the conception of the book as an object. Perhaps today there is greater commercial attention from the institutionality of art towards books as unique or exclusive objects, due to a multiplicity of variables. If we look back to the 19th century or the beginning of the 20th century, we already find examples of object-books or artist books, often conceived as such (perhaps with another name for the time, but understanding their contributions that comment on or investigate topics of interest to their authors) and others adjusted to the technological or economic limitations of their time. That's still the case. I am referring, for example, to books like *British Algae: Cyanotype Impressions* (1843) by Anna

Atkins or *La Boîte verte* (1934) by Marcel Duchamp. The list is long.

But one could also think that books have a very long history: there is a book called *El infinito en un junco. La invención de los libros en el mundo antiguo* (2019) by Irene Vallejo, which masterfully relates the history of books with knowledge and forms of political coexistence. So, the question could be whether we consider artist's books, book-objects or so-called photobooks part of that complex, diverse and amazing history of the ways in which ideas materialised on paper and other materials, or do they run in a different lane? If we understand editorial practices based on visuality (images, imaginaries, photographs, etc.) as narrative proposals, procedural ideas, intellectual sketches, and knowledge, we could propose that, since the invention of the technical image and advances in reproducibility, publications structured by visuality – artistic practices – could be a sociocultural response, a new way of communicating and apprehending existence.

So, rather than stopping at the "works/objects", we could think that these photobooks or those book-objects should inhabit public libraries, bookstores, home shelves, and classrooms as a form of constellation, where multiple stories and narratives that make up the world which we co-inhabit can fit. So, what would be the meaning of the shift towards the book as an object? For me, cataloguing the book as an object is a reduction of all its possibilities: artistic, intellectual, political, poetic, and material. It is pointing out the product-object over the possibilities that editorial practices have in contributing thinking about other possible worlds, or in opening up questions that can help us be more reflective and critical. I like categories less and less, especially those that govern the ways of establishing a relationship with the arts and creation. I think it is a contradiction, both intellectually and politically.

*What is the place of language and writing in a book of photographs?*

The role of language within a photobook depends entirely on the conception of the project. There is no set rule for how much writing should accompany images. For me, artistic creation is a way of generating knowledge, and that knowledge may require various tools, media and languages to be communicated. The relationship between text and image is inseparable; there are books where a single image can be enough to build a visual narrative, whilst, in other cases, the text is essential to give depth and context to what you want to convey. Or, also, images are always thought, and words are imagined.

For example, in the research we carried out in *Una revisión al fotolibro*, we included the book *Chile Ayer Hoy*, published in Santiago de Chile by Editorial Nacional Gabriela Mistral in 1975, a propaganda publication made at the beginning of the Chilean civil-military dictatorship. It proposes, amongst other things, a setting on the page: on the left, monochrome photographs on a black background exemplifying the "yesterday" of the Unidad Popular, whilst on the right, on a white background, the responses of the military junta that would be "today". The countless double pages were accompanied by information in Spanish, English and French. A trilingual book worked graphically under the prism of the binary: yesterday's evil on one of its pages is accompanied by the text 'Many students painted slogans in the service of Moscow' vs. today's good: 'Students help each other with their homework'. Three years later, seven volumes appeared, published by the Vicaría de la Solidaridad, an organisation dependent on the Catholic Church that defended human rights. All of them are titled *Dónde están?* (*'Where are they?'*), and are the compilation of data and information collected on disappearances due to repressive forces of the dictatorship. Inside, relevant information, relevant biographical data, circumstances of the disappearance, on the cover's portraits of some of the hundreds of missing men and women. These publications have a review in issue No9 of the South American magazine *Sueño de la Razón.*

*Who have been the models or templates for your own activities?*

Over the years, my students have become my greatest teachers. They always arrive with the same freshness, with current ideas that make me rethink my way of looking at the world. I also find inspiration in libraries. In my childhood home, there were always literary books, encyclopedias and cookbooks, which allowed me, from an early age, to understand the importance of those objects that opened new worlds. Today, I am still surrounded by books that allow me to inhabit a deeper time, something that is difficult to find in the immediacy of modern life.

The people who have expanded my horizons are those who, through their reflective thinking, have shown me the relevance of unlearning traditional historical narratives, both at a macro and micro level. It is essential to critically reflect on the stories we have inherited, the imaginaries that have been established, and the stories that exist – silenced or omitted – beyond the stories of power and violence.

*What's currently on your desk?*

My workspace reflects the constantly evolving process I am in. Notepads, whose pages I sometimes do not even understand afterwards, take up a large part of my desk. My agenda is essential in organising my ideas and daily life, whilst books, always present, open new perspectives and connections. I always read several books simultaneously: amongst them today on my nightstand are *Los cien nombres de América* (1991) by Miguel Rojas Mix and *inutilidad: el arte como educación* (2024) by Luis Camnitzer.

# NayanTara Gurung Kakshapati

NayanTara Gurung Kakshapati lives and works in Kathmandu, Nepal. She is the Co-Founder and Artistic Director of photo.circle, Nepal Picture Library and PhotoKTM – platforms and initiatives that nourish image-making, history-telling and dialogic engagements with diverse publics. As a cultural organiser and curator, she collaborates with photographers, filmmakers, researchers, writers, translators, educators, designers, organisers, and other professionals from various fields, to develop multidisciplinary exhibitions, publications, commissions, workshops, co-productions, and cultural tools. She is committed to creating possibilities for people who think, make, speak and organise in different ways to come together in 'imperfect solidarity' to learn, question, disrupt, and resist but also work towards repair.

*What is your process for arriving at decisions about
books and the projects that you undertake?*

The first book project I worked on at photo.circle was in 2010. We
titled the book *Hamra Hajurama* ('*Our Grandmothers*'). The book
featured stories of 12 grandmothers produced by seven photographers
and six writers. We initiated the project to be able to work together
as photographers and writers, to tell stories together. In many ways,
it was a response to the hierarchies that we were experiencing as
photographers and writers – in newsrooms, in spaces of knowledge
production, where writers were almost always put in charge of shaping
the narrative and photographers were expected to simply tag along
to do the visual illustrations. We designed the project in a way where
photographers and writers got to spend time together to get to know
each other and discuss ideas together, on equal footing. We then
paired up and worked on one or two stories each. Some of us already
knew each other, and some of us only knew each other's work. We
tried to make room for open exchanges. I was making pictures then
myself, and I got to work with Diwas Raja Kc for the first time. I forget
how we did the pairing – maybe we pulled names out of a hat! Diwas
and I travelled to Bardiya together to meet Sundari Devi Badi who
spoke to us about her struggles with and her relationship to land as
a Badi (Dalit) woman. It has been a long journey of being collaborators
since. I also got to work with Prawin Adhikari on a second story for
this project and we have continued to work together too. We
eventually presented the stories produced as an exhibition and also
made a book. This is typically how things have worked for us at photo.
circle – we have ideas, stories, questions, methods we want to pursue,
we find some resources, and then we launch into these experiments.
Over the years, we have made exhibitions and books to essentially
create space to tell stories and engage with different publics.

    After our initial collaboration in 2010, Diwas left to go back to
school. He came back in 2016 and we invited him to join us at Nepal
Picture Library. *DALIT: A Quest for Dignity* (2018) came about as an
archival campaign that he initiated and led, aiming to visibilise the
Nepali caste experience. It became an exhibition and a book. I went
to Delhi to make that book as we were quite frustrated with the
limited printing, paper binding options available to us in Kathmandu.
Sohrab Hura, a close friend and collaborator, had started printing his
books at Naveen Printers in Okhla and so I took his advice and

went there to explore options. I was amazed to see the production possibilities – the initial meeting was exhilarating but also a bit daunting. Sohrab said I should tell the printer exactly what I wanted, but I didn't really know! It was a great adventure, and a big learning experience for me. Despite the travel and transport costs, we have realised that it costs us less to print books in India.

We invited Kishor Sharma to make a book of his Raute work because we had been working with Kishor as he developed this work for almost 10 years. In 2019 we had the good fortune to meet the wonderful Valentina Abenavoli (thanks to Sohrab) who came into our lives like a shooting star. She has opened up so many new possibilities in the magical world of bookmaking for us. She ran a 10-day book making workshop in 2019 that Kishor participated in. He worked on his first dummy in that workshop. Several years passed, a few people saw the dummy and then it sat on a shelf, the work was showing here and there. In late 2020, some funding arrived and it felt like a very good time to share Kishor's work on the Rautes with a wider public. The Rautes are the last nomadic people of Nepal. They do not own land and have refused to accept citizenship offered to them by the Nepali state. Through *Living in the Mist* (2022) Kishor gives us an intimate glimpse into their lives and how they are resisting being governed by the 'modern' state. It compels us to imagine the possibility of alternative and autonomous ways of living. Kishor and Valentina worked online on the book design for more than a year. Towards the end of 2021, I ended up making several trips to Delhi again to get the book printed. The book is moving slowly – it is one of the most important works we have published till date.

*How do you like to work with people?*

I enjoy working collaboratively very much. I feel grateful for the energy, ideas, skills that folks, other than myself, bring to projects. I always feel more fulfilled by projects that have grown and evolved in these ways. They feel more rounded, more indexical, more nuanced. I have noticed that I opt for this mode quite immediately, and I find real joy in the work when things unfold in organically collaborative modes. I struggle between the 'I' and the 'we' as I think and speak about my/our work, as I'm doing through this text also, because sometimes it's impossible to tell where the 'we' ends and the 'I' begins and vice versa.

Having said all this, I have learnt that collaborative work must not be romanticised. We have been trying to work with a sharper awareness of the conditions and contexts within which collaborative work takes place, the power equations between collaborators that could be shaped by so many factors like age, gender, class, language, social and cultural capital, historical contexts, funding etc. Who has invited who into the collaboration, why, what are the shared motivations and shared convictions? Collaborative work requires the labour, ideas, knowledge, time, and skills of more than one person or group or institution. It asks us to let go of dominant ideas of authorship, ownership of ideas and knowledge and hierarchies between intellectual and other types of labour. Paradoxically, we are also of course still fighting long standing traditions of invisibilisation and exploitation of labour, appropriation of ideas and knowledge, and extractive modes of collaborations too. So how to work collaboratively is the question for me, not whether to or not.

photo.circle and the various initiatives that have emerged from this platform, have been experiments in collaborative, collective, institutional modes of working. Over time, we have learnt to ask the seemingly awkward and impolite questions – especially to bigger Western organisations who approach us – who does the partnership serve, how and why? How will the terms of working together be negotiated?

We have learnt that time and trust are key quotients, and so we try to take the time we need to build meaningful relationships with collaborators, instead of engaging in one offs.

We try not to become cynical. Long term collaborations with individuals as well as groups and institutions, have felt like hope giving solidarity projects when the conditions have been right, affirming our belief that collective work is the only way to liberation.



When it comes to books, we have attempted all sorts of forms and qualities. Big books, small books, cheap books, impressive books, non-threatening books. Some books we have made on cheap and local papers, and sold at very low prices (300 NPR/$2.5). We tried to distribute these small cheap photobooks at local bookshops, including the ones that sell stationery and textbooks. We were curious to see if we could find new markets and new networks away from the photobook circuits. Some books we have chosen to go with much higher quality paper and production – *DALIT: A Quest for*

*Dignity* was one of those projects. This was a project attempting to visibilise the caste experience of Nepali Dalits and insist that Dalit cultural practices constitute rich cultural heritage. It was a dignity project. We wanted the book to be beautiful to hold and look at. *The Public Life of Women –
A Feminist Memory Project* (2023) was also a special project but in a slightly different way. We made this book with Valentina and it has been a big, beautiful labour of love. We wanted the book to be portable, small enough to slip into a handbag, light enough to travel with many copies.

Access is determined by both affordability but also modes of circulation. We struggle with the circulation part. There are no ready made distribution channels for us in Nepal for the types of experimental books we are making. We self-distribute and yes that limits access. The print run for *The Public Life of Women – A Feminist Memory Project* was 2000 and we are down to our last 55 copies in little over one year. We distributed more than half the copies we printed, to the contributors to the Feminist Memory Project at no cost, as well as to schools, colleges and libraries. We really wanted to open up access to not only the book, but also the archive at large. We are currently planning a second reprint of *The Public Life of Women – A Feminist Memory Project* in collaboration with a more established publisher. We are hoping it can be accessible more widely then, and also sold.



We have always thought of the Nepali public as our primary audience – for the books we make, but also everything else we do. Our books and exhibitions are always bilingual – in both Nepali and English. Of course, we are also happy for the world to find our work and engage with it. Friends and strangers have told me that they have given our books to small libraries, to feminist organiser friends around the world, to teachers, to photographers, to their mothers – the thought of these books making their way into all these private and public realms, across many kinds of borders, makes my heart sing!



Photobooks are windows into many different worlds. They are certainly more portable than exhibitions. They can travel from bookshelf to

bookshelf, drawing invisible threads between our many worlds.
So yes, absolutely, they should reach other continents. Of course,
we have all had our share of distribution challenges to actually make
this possible. I have seen a few photographers and small publishers
work really hard to self-distribute and show us that it is possible to be
nimble and persistent and get one's work out by devising alternate
distribution mechanisms that do work – but it isn't easy and it can
become quite consuming to manage correspondence with bookshops
and folks who wish to buy directly, pack, ship, track and follow up on
payments etc. For us in Nepal, accessing online payment gateways
and receiving payments from outside the country is a challenge.
Cheaper shipping options are unreliable – many books and prints get
returned and services like DHL are very expensive – people often end
up having to pay more for shipping than for the book. I know other
friends across South Asia also struggle with this.

*What is the place of language and writing in a book of
photographs?*

Images can do things that text cannot, and vice versa. Writing can
provide expanded context for images, raise questions and concerns
around image-making practices, and situate images, how they are
made and used historically, politically, economically. Similarly, images
can add expanded visual nuance, information, emotion, and meaning
to written language. Images and text are greatly complementary
mediums. That does not mean that every book needs both all the time.

*Who have been the models or templates for your own
activities?*

For the most part, we have been making up our own ways of
working. We operate within increasingly transdisciplinary, flexible
and responsive frameworks and this has kept us going. We work
within many limitations so we have learnt how to duck and dive and
swerve as needed. It has been a lot of learning by doing. It has taken
some time to gain confidence in the fact that this is perhaps how
resilient institutions and initiatives survive and thrive. Over the years,
we have of course met many individuals and institutions whose work
we have respected and who we have learnt from and been inspired by.
Amongst them are all our friends and colleagues at Pathshala, Drik

and Chobi Mela International Photography Festival in Bangladesh.
We first met Shahidul [Alam] in 2007 or 2008 which was when we first
set up photo.circle and he has been a generous friend and mentor.
He then introduced us to many in his community and since then our
Bangla-bondhus have been close collaborators. After attending
several editions of Chobi Mela since 2008, we saw what a festival can
do for a photography community and so we set up PhotoKTM in 2015.
We have worked closely with Pathshala and run several exchange
programs collaboratively every year, however we realised that setting
up a formal photography school would not make sense for us as we
operate at a much smaller scale and so we run many teaching/learning
initiatives but chose not to set up a full-fledged photography school.
This has been a good decision for us as it has allowed us to do many
other things despite being a small team. So like this, we have been
taking inspiration from many models, templates and initiatives, but
picking and choosing so that what we adopt, makes sense for our
context. In more recent times, we have been taking inspiration from
many organisations, initiatives and individual practitioners such as the
Indonesian KUNCI Study Forum and Collective, the District Six
Museum in Cape Town, New Delhi based artist Amar Kanwar, Anadolu
Kultur based in Istanbul, Green Papaya from the Philippines, Panther's
Paw Publication based in Nagpur, India, the Iyatsiba Lab at the Centre
for Humanities Research (CHR) at University of Western Cape (UWC)
in South Africa, amongst others. We know some of these people and
initiatives and have had opportunities to collaborate and learn from
them. Others we know from a distance.

*What would make a better photobook ecosystem?*

Well, a lot of our challenges have to do with inequities in the world
I suppose. I would love to come together to think more about how
we can share resources and infrastructure between people making
books, small publishers, big publishers, bookshops and other points
of sale? Could we consider decentralised production, could we share
warehousing and tables at book fairs and bookshelves and bank
accounts, could we try barter systems that would allow us to
circumvent international banking and shipping hurdles?

# Bruno Ceschel

Bruno Ceschel is the Director of Self Publish, Be Happy (SPBH), an organisation dedicated to visual culture, education, and community. Since 2010, SPBH has staged events at institutions such as Tate Modern, MoMA PS1 and Kunsthal Charlottenborg. Its collection of over 3000 self-published photobooks is housed at the Maison Européenne de la Photographie (MEP) in Paris, France. As Publishing Director at SPBH Editions, Ceschel has published works by authors including Vince Aletti, Carmen Winant, Charlie Engman, and Claudia Rankine. He is a visiting lecturer at École cantonale d'art de Lausanne (ECAL) in Lausanne, Switzerland, and Cornell University in Ithaca, New York, US.

*What were the encounters which started your relationship
with photobooks?*

I got my first job as an intern, and later as an editor, at *COLORS*,
the publication founded by Tibor Karman and Oliviero Toscani. At the
time, it was edited by photographers Adam Broomberg and Oliver
Chanarin, and I don't think I had ever encountered a photobook
before working there.

During that period, they collaborated with Gigi Giannuzzi of
Trolley Books on *Ghetto* (2003), a book compiling much of the work
they had produced at *COLORS*. I contributed to that publication,
which was likely the first time I both worked on a photobook and
engaged with a photobook publisher. When I moved to London,
Trolley Books was a major player in what was then still a small, tightly
connected photobook world. Gigi was working with many remarkable
artists, and Trolley's gallery space on Redchurch Street was not just a
workspace but a social hub, with wild parties.

The act of making books was never just about publishing – it was
about creating a network of interesting people and a community
around the work, something I carried forward throughout my career.
That scene was my first real exposure to the photobook community
before I eventually joined Chris Boot, just as he was launching his own
imprint. Both Gigi and Chris were pivotal in shaping my interest and
understanding of photobooks – not just as objects, but as platforms
for ideas and communities.

*What is your process for arriving at decisions about
books and the projects you undertake?*

At SPBH Editions, a book isn't just a product – it's a potential active
agent of change. Every project we take on has to be urgent, vital and
necessary. I'm not interested in publishing books that simply
document or preserve; a book has to act, to push forward a
conversation, shift perspectives or challenge the dominant narratives
that shape the way we think, see and live. This feels even more urgent
now, in a moment that is possibly the most troubling in my lifetime.
More than ever, we need writers, artists and academics to resist and
rethink the world being imposed on us, to offer alternative ways of
seeing, imagining and acting.

This balance has shifted over time. Early in my career, I was primarily publishing for myself and my immediate community – people who already understood the artistic language I was working within. Economics played a role, of course, but I wasn't overly concerned with reaching a broad audience.

That has changed – not just because of financial realities, but because I now see my role as ensuring that the books, ideas and authors I support reach beyond the expected circles. The challenge is making complex, layered ideas accessible without diluting their essence. I often think about this in terms of design and marketing – the book as a honey trap. It should look inviting, sexy, accessible on the surface, but once inside, the reader encounters something challenging, thought provoking.



I studied sociology in London in the late 1990s, at a time when globalisation was seen as a force for greater equality – a potential bridge rather than a dividing line. Of course, we've since learned that this isn't entirely true, but that early perspective shaped the way I think. Though that optimism has faded, the idea that books – and ideas – should move freely has stayed with me. I grew up with a strong sense of being European, but also with the belief that culture and conversations shouldn't be confined by borders. I never saw myself as catering to one specific community, country or audience – I didn't then, and I don't now. My approach to publishing has always been rooted in a global mindset.

When I think about this, I think, for example, of the work of Carmen Winant. The first book we published with her, *My Birth* (2018), was deeply personal – reflecting her own experience of childbirth – whilst also in dialogue with a larger history of birth, representation and collective experience. The book interwove found images of other women's births, creating a resonance that transcended the personal and spoke to audiences across the globe. Even more explicitly, *The Last Safe Abortion* (2024), which we recently published with Carmen, was created in response to the overturning of Roe v. Wade, the landmark US ruling that had previously protected the constitutional right to abortion. The book documents the last remaining abortion clinics in the Midwest, just before some of them were forced to shut down, situating it in the longer, ongoing struggle for reproductive rights. Whilst the book focuses on a specific legal and political moment in the US, its impact extends far beyond that – touching on broader conversations about bodily autonomy, access to care and reproductive freedom worldwide.

The books I publish engage with specific places, histories and identities, but always as part of a larger, interconnected conversation. Whilst certain issues are deeply local, they resonate across geographies and lived experiences.

What do you think is the significance of the shift towards the book as an object?

Engaging with photographs – and, I would argue, the pleasure of reading text – is intrinsically tied to the printed page. I started my career just as the internet began reshaping how content is disseminated and, over time, the contrast between physical books and digital consumption has become more pronounced. The tactility of books, their permanence and their role as carefully crafted experiences have only grown more significant.

Because of this, the book as an object has become central to contemporary publishing. Of course, I care about materials, printing techniques and ensuring images are reproduced as artists envision them, but I also think about books more expansively. A book can take the form of a poster, a zine, a pamphlet – it doesn't have to be a high-end, collectible art object. Too often, the "book-as-object" is associated with luxury, exclusivity and pristine production. But the form itself can be fluid – it's about creating something that demands to be engaged with, held and lived with. Some books are intimate and small, designed to be carried, annotated and passed between hands. Others assert themselves with sheer physical presence, refusing to be ignored.

One book that has accompanied me through various homes and countries, and now resides on my coffee table, is *Surrendered Myself to the Chair of Life* (2012) by Jin Ohashi, published by AKAAKA Art Publishing. This work stands as one of the most incredible and confounding books I've ever encountered. Enormous in scale and housed within a box, it defies simple categorisation. The book presents a twisted sequence of images, culminating in a choreographed orgy of hundreds of individuals. Its form and structure are integral to its meaning – it is simultaneously a book and a sculpture, challenging the act of reading and demanding a physical, almost performative engagement. Navigating through its pages is deliberately difficult, reinforcing the idea that the book itself is an experience, not just a container for images.



Beyond making mindful material choices, I think sustainability in publishing is about responsible production – that is, only making books that need to exist. This means being deliberate about print runs, ensuring books don't languish in storage or become waste. I've also been focusing more on co-production in different territories, especially for text-based books. Partnering with local publishers allows us to minimise shipping and air freight, significantly reducing our environmental footprint. Instead of moving books across the world, we can produce them where they are needed, making distribution more efficient and sustainable. Publishing will never be perfectly sustainable, but we can make smarter, more conscious choices at every stage of the process.



A new generation of publishers.
I came up in the late 2000s, at a time when there was a wave of independent publishers and self-publishers entering the scene. We joined an existing market alongside established names like Steidl, Aperture and Thames & Hudson. Some of those indie publishers have since grown into major players, but I think the next evolution of the ecosystem depends on a fresh wave of small, independent publishers – voices that will bring new perspectives, new life experiences and new geopolitical viewpoints.
The photobook world remains heavily Westernised, and a healthier ecosystem would mean greater diversity – not just in the kinds of books being published, but in who is publishing them. New publishers can challenge existing norms, introduce alternative publishing models and push the medium forward in unexpected ways.

Publishing needs new energy, new urgencies and new geographies – otherwise, we'll just keep repeating ourselves.



I don't really have a desk. In the office, we have a huge table – a space for sequencing images, reviewing material and holding meetings, but also a kind of communal workspace. It's not a place where I keep any personal objects, as it's constantly shifting to accommodate different projects. I also find myself traveling a lot, splitting my time between Milan and London, so I don't really have a personal desk or a fixed workspace of my own.

There is, however, one object that has been sitting there for a while, and perhaps it's significant in illustrating how I work. A couple of months ago, I was at a second-hand market and came across a 1942 edition of *Più che l'amore*, a theatre script by Gabriele D'Annunzio. I was drawn to it not because of the content – I don't particularly care for D'Annunzio's work and will likely never read it – but because of the design, the typography and the title, which translates to '*More than love*'. There was something in the rationalist aesthetic of the cover that intrigued me, and I bought it without knowing exactly why.

I often find myself collecting images, books or objects that don't have an immediate use, yet seem to lodge themselves somewhere in my thinking. Sometimes, I save images to my digital desktop, sometimes I hold onto a book like this, unsure of what it means but knowing that, over time, it might inform the way I think, imagine or create. This process – of intuitively gathering things before I understand their significance – is very much part of how I work.

# Paul Ninson

Paul Ninson is an educator, scholar, curator,
photographer, and cultural practitioner. In 2022 he
established Africa's biggest photography library,
nested within Dikan Center, Accra, Ghana, a non-profit
institution dedicated to shaping the next generation of
Africa's creative leaders. Having witnessed firsthand the
impact of young African photographers and creatives being
denied resources, Ninson's mission is to impact lives
through the transformative power of visual education.
He continually strives to make visual education
accessible for all through educational programmes,
curating exhibitions, cultural heritage and archiving,
as well as community engagement.

It all began with my love for books and reading, an infection from my father. Reading was a big part of my upbringing, whether it was the Bible or Ladybird books. Photobooks were my first love and go-to for inspiration and learning when I began my photography journey. Oral stories from my grandparents exposed me to the art of storytelling, and I guess photography was the best medium for me to express myself more fully. The emergence of a photobook culture at the Dikan Center is deeply rooted in the need for equity and accessibility to knowledge, specifically African knowledge, for creatives in Ghana and beyond. It was extremely hard to access books and materials on photography and visual culture in Africa. To be an African visual storyteller, it is important to know African visual history. I remember the shock I felt when I got to New York, seeing so many African materials in various libraries yet not accessible in Ghana or other parts of Africa. These encounters influenced my quest to build the Dikan ecosystem as a way of educating the African creative leader.

The impetus to establish the Dikan Center was to educate through books, materials and programming. Photobooks here are not just collections of photographs, but curated experiences that reflect the complexities and beauty of African life. This dedication to cultivating a photobook culture is about affirming the value of our stories and ensuring they resonate not just within Africa, but globally, thus bridging cultural gaps and fostering a deeper understanding of the continent and its history.



The history of photobooks in Africa has greatly influenced my initiative to create Africa's first and largest photographic library. Initially, photobooks in Africa were mainly produced by outsiders during the colonial era, focusing on ethnographic views that didn't truly reflect African life. However, post-independence, African photographers began using photobooks to showcase their own stories and culture, which inspired me. Seeing how African photographers like Seydou Keïta and Malick Sidibé, as well as contemporary artists such as Zanele Muholi, have used photobooks to challenge stereotypes and celebrate African identities motivated me to create a space in which this rich heritage could be preserved and appreciated widely. This led to the establishment of a library that not only houses photobooks but also supports a broader understanding of African visual culture. Through this library, my goal has been to make African visual culture accessible to both Africans and the global community, promoting exhibitions, research and educational programmes that expand on the narratives these photobooks offer. This initiative is about honouring our past whilst shaping a future narrative that reflects the true diversity and dynamism of African cultures.

The guiding principles for selecting and sourcing at the Dikan Center are deeply rooted in our mission to reflect the true diversity and richness of the continent's knowledge systems. We prioritise works that offer new insights, challenge stereotypes and fill knowledge gaps in African visual history. Each selection is considered for its potential to contribute significantly to educational programmes, stimulate scholarly research and enhance public understanding of art and culture. We seek to increase the African collection, despite the considerable financial costs.

*How do you balance choices between working with highly specific materials or processes, and the desire for access?*

The motivation to start our own publishing programme stemmed from a critical look at the global publishing landscape, where African voices were significantly underrepresented. By establishing a dedicated publishing programme, we are able to support African photographers, researchers and writers in creating works that authentically represent their cultures and stories. This initiative also stems from a desire to have control over the narratives we share, ensuring that they are told with the dignity and depth that is often missing from outside portrayals of Africa.

The state of photobook publishing in Africa is at a pivotal moment, characterised by a growing recognition of its value as a medium for storytelling. The future looks bright, as more institutions and initiatives like Dikan emerge to support and promote photobook projects. Photobooks serve as essential educational resources at Dikan, providing unique material for curatorial work, enriching our archives and supporting various educational and development programmes. They offer tangible insights and historical records that are indispensable for research and teaching.



The photobook, along with books and archival materials, is the cornerstone of Dikan's ecosystem, acting as both a documentation and preservation of African history. It captures the essence of eras, movements and changes across the continent, offering future generations a well-recorded and accessible history of indigenous knowledge systems.

The audience for our photobooks is incredibly diverse, encompassing anyone from scholars and students to artists and general readers across the globe. We specifically aim to engage those who are directly impacted by the narratives we present, including African communities and diasporas seeking connections with their respective heritages. Engagement with photobooks is on the rise in Africa, driven by an increasing appreciation for their role in preserving culture and history. Promoting their educational and aesthetic values is essential to building further interest and understanding of their significance.



International distribution is crucial not only for the sustainability of photobook projects but also for promoting cross-cultural understanding. As a curator and publisher, global distribution expands the impact of our work, enabling African stories to reach a worldwide audience and contribute to a more inclusive global narrative. Whilst continually aiming for international distribution, we also remain committed to maintaining a balance that respects and promotes localised value alongside global recognition.



Language and narrative are central to the impact of our photobooks and publications, providing essential context and depth to the visual content. The interplay between image and text in our books is carefully crafted to enhance the reader's understanding and engagement with the material. Whilst photobooks are powerful research tools, they are most effective when used in conjunction with other forms of media. For the most part, there isn't a great difference between my approach to curating an exhibition and creating a photobook, just as the text or captions for an exhibition, so as the text and images relate. This multimedia approach allows for a richer exploration of topics, inserting photobooks within a larger, more dynamic landscape that includes digital platforms, exhibitions and interactive archives. We are seeking to go beyond photobooks as a mere static form. I am currently working on a book on African music, in which I am including links to a dedicated website for other forms such as augmented reality, video and so on.

*Who have been the models or templates for your own activities?*

Influential figures in the field of photography and cultural preservation have greatly shaped my approach and vision for Dikan. Particularly, organisations such as the Walther Collection have been instrumental in highlighting the importance of preserving and showcasing African photography. These figures and institutions serve as benchmarks for our work at Dikan, inspiring our efforts to create a sustainable and impactful ecosystem of visual culture. We aspire for a fair world in which Africans can have equal access to African knowledge.

*What would make a better photobook ecosystem?*

Improvements could include greater support for local publishers, initiatives to foster collaborations across different media and increased funding and resources for publishing projects. As a publication and journal, Dikan Press can play a significant role here. Major publishers could have a profound impact by partnering with local institutions to co-publish and distribute photobooks, ensuring these publications are accessible and relevant locally whilst also reaching an international audience. This approach would not only amplify African voices but also enrich the global literary and artistic landscape with diverse African perspectives.

# Sohrab Hura

*Sohrab Hura is a photographer and filmmaker based in New Delhi, India. Recent exhibitions include:* Mother *(MoMA PS1, New York, US, 2024);* Ghosts in My Sleep *(Experimenter Colaba, Mumbai, India, 2023);* Spill *(Huis Marseille, Amsterdam, the Netherlands, 2021) and* Companion Pieces: New Photography *(MoMA, New York, 2020). Hura's work has been shown in international festivals such as Vancouver International Film Festival, Arkipel International Documentary and Experimental Film Festival, Jakarta, Indonesia, and FotoFest International, Houston, US. Hura was awarded the Paris Photo-Aperture Photobook of the Year Award for* The Coast *(2019) and nominated to the Paris Photo–Aperture PhotoBook of the Year Award for* Look It's Getting Sunny Outside!!! *(2018). His work is found in the permanent collection of MoMA, Ishara Art Foundation, Dubai and Cincinnati Art Museum, Ohio, US, amongst other private and public collections.*

In 2009, I didn't have a laptop and I had been asked to carry my work
along with me to show to people at a photo festival that I had been
invited to. In desperation, I sat up one night, a few days before
departure, and I made a book. It was the first draft of my book *Life Is
Elsewhere*. After seeing this first book maquette, I realised that my
photographs had turned into something else altogether. To fill up blank
pages, I started to write inside the book and gave the first copy of the
dummy to my mother who was still recovering from her relapse of an
illness. I had never spoken to her about what had gone on but the
book made it easy to say things that had felt difficult to say aloud.

This was not too long before I made my first film *Pati* (2010),
that had incorporated an amalgamation of photographs, film footage,
recorded sounds, text scribbled onto paper, and my voiceover
that read out a script I had written. The film, too, had been made
overnight by accident, after having incorrectly read a request for the
submission of material at the end of a grant period. Here, too, by the
time I had completed that short film, I had been left with a feeling
that the form of film could make images move in a manner that was
very different.

How do images move? Can they move as if weighed down by
slowness or can they rapidly hurtle towards the viewer? That for me
became the crux of my relationship with the book as well as whatever
other form I could experiment with images during that early period.

In 2009, the book was for me still a beautiful "fuck you"
to the exhibition form that had, at the time, felt a bit too precious.
But by the time I published my first book in 2015, that first feeling of
love for the form had already worn off because of all the noise around
the photobook. It's a weird relationship for me now. On the one hand,
I don't want to care about photobooks at all, but it's also the only
thing that comes to mind as something that I can give to someone
I am in love with. It is then at that moment that I truly appreciate
the photobook.

I love film projection in general because of its ephemerality.
But then again, I also make my exhibitions and projections and
whatever else as "book builders". It's a bit of a confused relationship.
Like many loves.

     *Sohrab Hura*

There is no fixed process as such. I often do this exercise with students in which I ask them to look around the room they are sitting in. I ask them to switch the lights off and to then feel their way about in the dark to make sense of the room. They often stretch their arms out in front to make sure that there is distance between them and any other obstacles. From initially seeing the room, they end up feeling the room. They might make their way along a wall and maybe their fingers come to know the texture of the wall which is something they may not have paid attention to when they could see the room. Maybe a crack or paint peeling off here and there. Maybe the wall feels damp and not as dry as it looked. Maybe their knee bumps against a chair that is out of place. Maybe they step on a coin that had fallen onto the floor. They might remember that they had seen the coin from the corner of their eye when the early morning sun shone into the room through the gap in between the window curtains. They had hit snooze on the first alarm and had decided that they would pick it up after 10 minutes of being cosy under the quilt. Their eyes had moved from the coin, lazily up to the sliver of the damp dewy window that peeked at them from in between the curtains. The crispy-ness of the weather outside reminded them of how, when it had got extremely cold the previous night, it had felt nice to hold hands with the person that they had gone out on a date with. In all of this reminiscing, they had forgotten about the coin entirely and continued to go about their day and the coin had remained on the floor. Now I ask them to switch the lights back on in their room. The room seems different to them now. The room now exists in multiple registers, many of which are beyond the register of plain sight.

For me, making work is a long series of switching the light of my room on and off. I have a rough inkling of what I want to do at first. Play is so important and I need to work as intuitively as possible, especially at the start. At some point, I start to collate together whatever I might have made to be able to get a sense of it at that moment, to see what patterns emerge. Usually, at the start, the work could be anywhere because the possibilities are many. And it can get tempting to catch on to the possibilities that seem more dominant but I don't want to commit to anything straight away because you never know how another thread which seems tiny at first might grow beautifully with time. So, I again get into this extended period of working intuitively and then I again collate everything together. This back-and-forth alternation between intuition and deliberation goes on with different patterns and directions. In a way, as this switching on and off the lights of the room goes on, it allows me to look within and outside the room. I can now look into the room from the outside and the other way around. I become more aware of how I'm looking at the room, or from the room. And so on... I'm no longer just looking at the room but I'm looking relatively towards the room.

On the question of what form my work will take: will it be a book or a film or an exhibition or all of it or something else altogether? All that starts to emerge on its own? It's quite organic really. Building the small start that I have into something bigger over time is what works for me. It's the only way I can remain curious and excited about my work throughout.

As time has passed, I have realised that making work or a photobook or whatever else is actually like any other ordinary process of building that I have undergone, even from the time when I was a kid. I'm often reminded of the time when I would fly kites. It would take a lot of huffing and puffing to get the kite going at first. I'd have to give rapid tugs to the string to get the kite off the ground. The kite would jerk upwards and downwards and sideways as if it was gasping for breath and my attention would be solely to not let it crash to the ground. And in between those short tugs, from to time I'd let the string slip out a little bit to let the kite gain some distance. The initial flight would require a lot of effort but, at some point, the kite would catch on to a breeze and start to soar. From here on, I wouldn't have to do much because the wind would carry it. But it was from this moment on that I'd start to watch for the tension on the string more carefully. The string would not let me feel how strong the wind in the sky would be. At some point, I'd start to worry that if I didn't reel the kite back in a little bit, the string would snap.

The more experience I'd gain at kite flying, the easier it would become for me to gauge the sky right at the start and figure out what knots to tie on the kite. If the sky was clear, then I'd often balance the knots equally so that the kite would remain calm. But if there were other kites in the sky, then I'd tie a knot that was a little out of balance so that the kite would spin wildly. That would give me the chance to outmaneuver the other kites by changing direction quickly at will and perhaps also allowing me to steal the other kite should I have emerged

     *Sohrab Hura*

as the victor in our engagement. Making books is a lot like flying kites. And the more books I make, the more familiar I become with the process of having an idea of what I might need for the next book, even before I make it. But each new kite still has to get off the ground in the first place.



D. Junisha Khongwir and Karen L. Donoghue are rare examples of artists who have really taken their book *Stories From The Valley* (2023) back into the communities which their book is addressing in an immensely generous way. I don't think I could manage to do what they have done. Their small book run ran out of print almost immediately with almost all books being distributed amongst the community who the stories were meant for. They wanted to make something that was beautiful but also bore down on maintaining the integrity of oral histories that they were recording. It's quite remarkable that they have done this and their book is one of the very few examples of books that went back almost entirely to the people who the books were made for.

My work, on the other hand, exists within a broader spectrum of audience. My mother's doctor, who has overseen her health for the last 25 years, has my first few books in which my mother is the protagonist, *Life Is Elsewhere* (2015) and *Look It's Getting Sunny Outside!!!* (2018). I had not thought of giving a book about my mother and her schizophrenia to a psychiatrist even though in hindsight it seems like such an obvious thing to do. But he had himself asked my mother for it. And it had less to do with the subject matter and more with the fact that he has known me from my teenage years when I'd visit my mother in the hospital and he has seen me grow up and figure my way out. I'm so glad he has them.

Many copies of my book *The Coast* (2019) have been distributed here in India itself. That book will for sure have a very different reading here than it might somewhere else. I'm glad to have copies of my books in general in different libraries and schools. And then there are the photobook collectors, but many of them in our region itself.

Whilst making the books, I do not think of any particular audience. Once I have arrived at a final draft of sorts, sometimes I think of building a bridge outwards. It's a bit like cooking where you finally temper the dish in the end. You might have invited many guests for a meal but you might temper it for a select few and that might set the tone and the taste for the rest of the guests. I guess this is also the role of making an address in many of my books. They may be addressed to specific people but, for me, it's like a bridge made for a specific person that somebody else can use to cross over as well.

I think I'm quite selfish in the way I look at books because I want to make them primarily for myself. But I hope that if it is vulnerable enough, someone else might recognise themselves in me.

*How important is it for photobooks to reach other continents?*

Earlier, when I'd self-publish, it mattered to me that the majority of the copies of my books remained here – "here" being in India, South Asia, South East Asia, East Asia, the larger Asian region, South America, countries in Africa, you know… "Here" for all of us is so different. I'd often have people from Europe, UK and the US write to me to complain about how my books are not easily available in their countries and cities. They'd tell me about how they have to order all the way from India or wait a long time for my books to reach the booksellers near them. There would often be a sense of entitlement leaking out from under the skin of those complaints – the entitlement to access.

The photobook scene is always made out to be in Paris or London or New York. We always see a centre somewhere else, mainly in the West, and decide what the history of the photobook is supposed to be, what book is to be celebrated and things like that, just like how we in Delhi and Bombay do it ourselves here in India, without much acknowledgement of what is happening elsewhere. For a long time, whilst we have watched such things play out from afar from "here", we have also struggled to get access to the very books that we have been told by the distant centre that we should have to look up to.

To be honest, when people would complain about my self-published books not being easily available in Europe or the UK or the US, I remember there would be a warm gooey feeling in my stomach and smile on my face. But recently, I published the book of drawings *Things Felt But Not Quite Expressed* (2024) with MACK and now my books are more easily available in the West than "here".

I don't want to simplify the answer to your question by saying something like: "Yes, photobooks should be able to reach other continents." Instead, I want to ask what these other continents are, and from which locations one asking or answering this question from. Maybe the answer might then be a bit more complicated.



At times, I feel that it's lovely that beautiful objects exist in this world because why not. But then, at other times, I just don't care about the book as an object so much. At the core of it, I enjoy a photobook that feels as fulfilling as a novel or a collection of short stories or poems that has remained close to my heart – you know, a kind of a book that we often hand over to someone we might recognise ourselves in. It doesn't matter if it's a paperback, or if the pages have got a little worn out. The words are enough to make the book sing. I have the desire of making a photobook like that kind of book. At least, that is where I always want to start from.

The physical objecthood of the photobook is an add-on that definitely plays its own role but I wouldn't want to ever foreground that characteristic in my desire to make a photobook because I would not want to risk reducing the book to only becoming something precious. Instead of looking at the book as an object, I like to engage with the making of the book from another side of the same prism of the "object", by thinking about the haptics of the book. How will someone hold the book? Will it feel to someone like it is their own if they were to hold it in their hand? How will the size of the book affect the pace of reading it, will the pace of the turning of pages increase or decrease depending on the size of the book? When I made *Life Is Elsewhere* and *Look It's Getting Sunny Outside!!!*, I wanted the book to fit into the reader's hand just like a diary might have. I wanted the weight of the book to play its own part in letting the person holding it walk with it, swinging their arms with lightness, a bit like when you do when you fall in love. A heavier book would have not allowed the reader to feel comfortable carrying it in one hand, let alone swinging their arms in love. The paper choice, the handwritten text, the covering of every book with archival mylar to make the cover feel a bit like glass, even though the inside of the book had a completely different surface of uncoated paper, were little nudges to the reader that I had hoped would loosen up the shoulders of whoever held the books in their hands. *Things Felt But Not Quite Expressed* is of a similar size as family albums that we had at home when I was growing up in the 1980s and 90s. The cover of the book is foam-padded and the book feels like a gooey book and not a hard back or soft-covered. I started to draw to look for softness and, whilst designing the book, I had hoped that the touch of the book would also feel soft. You know, the physical object echoing what resides within it, in this case. In a way, I want the objecthood of a book to play a role similar to what a score is to a film. It needs to do its magic in an invisible way.

Recently, in another interview, I had been asked an entirely different question but I feel that the answer to that question could also become the answer to the question that you asked about the shift towards the book as an object.

I had written about how I think about my work as a garden. When I leave my apartment, I cross many homes where people who love and care for plants live. In many of the houses that I pass, I see that people have lined up their plants neatly along the walls. The space between pot is carefully measured because that arrangement is meant to display a sense of harmony and symmetry. Nothing is supposed to look out of place. My garden at home which moves between my living room and my two balconies depending on the season is a little different, a little unkept in fact. Different plants are clustered together with leaves of one plant disappearing in between the leaves of another. It's a bit like a small grove that I can enter and sit in or draw or just be with my plants. It doesn't matter so much what it looks like from the outside, as long as it feels inviting enough for me or anyone else visiting to want to enter and be. But if it looks pretty from a distance, then that's nice as well.

So, in a way my relationship to "the book as an object" is also like my relationship with my garden. I'd want the reader of the book to want to feel like the guest who wants to sit inside the garden with the plants and not just look at it from a distance. I suppose in that sense, the physical objecthood of the book is something that I might arrive at from the inside out.



I don't think of a photobook as being the same as a book of photographs. I think of the photobook as a kind of logic – a logic with which I build something. It isn't simply just the physical object itself.

     *Sohrab Hura*

A photobook is an idea, a perspective more than anything else. We could say that the photobook is a language itself. And language is not limited to only text and speech. So, the question you ask does not make sense to me.

You do whatever you have to do to get wherever you want to get to. Photographs, writing and whatever else that you might use are just raw material.

*What would make a better photobook ecosystem?*

I don't know. I feel like I've lost touch with the photobook scene to some extent over the last few years. It's been so good for me to keep some distance between myself and the on-goings of the photobook ecosystem. I'm sure somebody else in this series will manage to give you a clear and definite answer to this question.

*What's currently on your desk?*

Paint.

# Ivan Vartanian

*Ivan Vartanian has edited and authored numerous books on photography and art, including* Japanese Photography Magazines: 1880s to 1980s *(Goliga, 2023)* Japanese Photobooks of the 1960s & '70s *(Aperture, 2009),* Setting Sun: Writings by Japanese Photographers *(Aperture, 2005), among others.*

My mother was an amateur watercolourist who painted dancers. She used books of ballet and contemporary dance as references. That was my first introduction to the illustrated book. Fast forward, I'm at NYU and, at that time, art books were wrapped in Saran Wrap and sold on the sidewalks of Manhattan – because, you know, they were stolen. I bought a lot of art books that way. One was Robert Mapplethorpe's *Lady Lisa Lyon*. I planned to use it as a drawing reference. That was my first encounter with a proper photography book. Around that time, at a proper bookstore, I saw *The Ballad of Sexual Dependency* by Nan Goldin (1986). Just by happenstance, when I graduated I saw an internship available at this place called Aperture – I had never heard of it. I applied and became the intern (it was called 'work scholar') of the Senior Editor, Melissa Harris. That is where a few months later I met Nan Goldin!

At Aperture, I was blown away by the people that I met. Melissa, if you ever have the great pleasure of meeting her, is a force of nature; she's one of those super humans. Michael Hoffman, who was the former Director and worked with Minor White, was more like a tornado. Because of them, I met Merce Cunningham and Meredith Monk; John Waters called me; Paul Auster sent me packages. On and on and on like this. I met amazing performance artists. It was an experience of seeing how this thing, that was making photobooks, was a passport, a conduit, into meeting these people who were radically different from everything I knew growing up in New York. Books themselves were not so much a thing as it was the possibility of engaging these godlike people. I remember meeting Nan Goldin for the first time. She strode into the office looking like she had walked off a movie set of a period piece set in Berlin. Her wine-coloured leather coat went all the way past her knees and she wore high-heeled boots. She was so strikingly self-assured.

Plus, the staff at Aperture were smart and erudite. I met Lesley A. Martin, who had a Kawasaki motorcycle, blue hair; she'd been living in Japan, and could read and write Japanese. Meanwhile, you know, I knew nothing. I was exposed to nothing until then. Aperture had an amazing in-house library and I went through every single book. There were books from Japan too. One day, a book arrived from some chap called Daido Moriyama. The title was *Daido Hysteric, No.7*. It was so different from everything that we were doing at Aperture. Our books had a lot of big, white borders, serif typefaces, and captions. At Aperture, we worked with exhibition prints: our job was to make sure that we, as faithfully as possible, reproduced the quality of those darkroom prints on the printed page. The exhibition print was always the artefact that we were copying. Moriyama's book was so un-precious: the paper was really glossy; you touch it and your fingerprints got on it and bent easily. The photographs were at odd angles and went into the gutter; it was full bleed; there were no chapters, no page numbers, no explanation, nothing. At that time there was a lot of interest in Japan, which was thought of as a different world, like an alternate universe: *Ghost in the Shell* came out, and I was reading Murakami Takashi before Murakami Haruki. I saw Oe Kenzaburo read one of his texts at a Barnes & Noble on Park Avenue South. It was a series of mind-expanding experiences and it was this miraculous confluence. Through Aperture, a Japanese publisher of art books offered me a job. I packed my bags and landed in Tokyo a few months later. That was nearly 30 years ago.

That was what led me to photobooks: the life that it represented, the exposure, and how it was a gateway into a different world. Getting involved with producing books happened later: I had started book projects while I was working for a Japanese publisher, and they went bankrupt. I still had all these projects, and Distributed Art Publishers/D.A.P. said to me, "Why don't you package the books for us? We'll just buy them from you." I asked, "What's packaging?". That was the start of my entrepreneurial journey: I began making books and selling them directly to the distributors, and that continued for quite a number of years. Then I realised that I wasn't just – I don't know how to say it in English – *henpuro* – a gun-for-hire editor: I wasn't merely packaging things and selling them. I was editing, and then I was also authoring, and then it evolved into me being the author. Later, I started working with artists to create projects that didn't necessarily have the book as the final output.

*How do you like to work with people?*

He wasn't my professor in an official capacity, but I consider Kaneko Ryuichi my teacher. Everything that I know about Japanese photography initially came through him. I was very much at the feet of a giant, absorbing every single word that he said. His word was

     *Ivan Vartanian*

scripture to me. That relationship lasted until he died in 2021. After that, I felt adrift. I thought, 'Well, that's it for me making books about Japanese photography.' My relationship with writing historical books has changed dramatically since the magazine book [*Japanese Photography Magazines: 1880s to 1980s*], in that the assertions I make are now entirely my responsibility. There's no grand teacher to whom I can defer. And that is the fundamental difference between what I used to do, what I have done until now, and what I am doing going forward.

With artist's books [the imprint Goliga], it is very much me pitching ideas to the artist, followed by a back-and-forth of *yes, no, yes, no, yes, no, yes, no, yes, no, yes, no, yes, no*, until we reach a point where the collaboration becomes very fluid. With Takano Ryudai, if you observe from the outside, it might appear as though I'm directing him, but we have an exceptionally fluid rapport, and when working on something, I'll push his hand away, or he'll push my hand away. We don't even think about it. With the other artists I work with, it's always a sense of camaraderie: very casual initially, then it evolves into something meaningful. There needs to be some kind of established dialogue, or way of working with each other that fosters comfort and trust.



Going forward with the books and multiples, I want to focus on much smaller editions, limited to about 10 copies at most. The specific approach will depend on the technique and materials, but I plan to implement timed releases. Alternatively, I might offer an open edition that's only available for order during a three-month window, after which production will permanently cease. I'm also exploring pre-sales models, where I would only produce the orders I've received in advance. The financial calculations and logistical considerations of sales and production are now directly informing my choices of techniques and materials. Previously, I took a much more open-ended approach, which occasionally led to difficulties with overproducing certain items and underproducing others.

It's very challenging to accurately assess the market, especially at an ambiguous price point. For $1,000, you could potentially purchase a small photographic print from a gallery, but that same amount could alternatively buy 10 vintage books or five exceptional vintage volumes. Each production decision involves considerable risk. I'll work within these parameters as best I can. I want to avoid creating photo books, because there are specialists like Michael Mack who excel in that area. Similarly with monographs: there are established publishers already focused on that format. I don't need to compete in or replicate paths that others have already developed. I'm more interested in exploring the inherent power of books as objects. I'm particularly drawn to creating books that blur the boundary between illustration and photographic plate, integrated with text. I'm investigating approaches where the image functions as a graphical element, serving an illustrative purpose on the page. An extreme reference point would be publications like Benetton's *COLORS* magazine, or even propaganda materials.

I think there is room in the world to organise groups of people around the cause of making books that mean something to them as a community. And that is what I'm interested in doing as another part, a new avenue in my practice of teaching editorial design, and the practice of publishing as a community building, community organising event. I think that has a lot of real-world practical applications. For now, it's a project I'm calling Book Bureau.

*How important is it for photobooks to reach other continents?*

Oh, why bother otherwise?

With the history books, my goal is to have them in public libraries, so that they are accessible for free to whoever wants to see them. I go after librarians at universities, museums and public libraries, and regional libraries. I literally write to librarians all the time: "Please know about this book. I will offer you free shipping if you're a public collection". It is very important. I have inventory in the US. I have inventory in France. I have inventory in Japan. It's very important for these books to travel. You know, the Japanese Photography Magazine book, for example, is $100, $105. I have put a lot of effort into getting it into a public collection, where with a library card, you can access it for free. So, say what you want about the retail price. Librarians are my target, because you want them in permanent collections around the world, catalogued, indexed, accessible. Second are educators and academics, because they refer books to their libraries, to their institutions. Also, I want to make sure that they are equipped to teach, to use these books as a teaching resource. Third are curators, alongside magazines. Really, I'm here to serve librarians and regular people who crazily have $100 to spend on this super niche subject.



I think they're one and the same. I think the choice in how to publish something determines its audience. It is part and parcel of the editorial and authoring process. It always amazes me when artists and photographers and writers forfeit foundational decisions to other people because they don't have, as they say, a platform. If you don't have your own platform you don't have your own audience and you're relying on someone else's audience to get into the world. If you are just going to a publisher to deposit your content and push it out to sales venues, that's not the conversation I'm interested in having. Making books means you are communicating with multiple people, and you have a responsibility to that audience and you want to be in connection with them in some form, in a dialogue, listening to their needs, and then fulfilling those needs. It is definitely a give and take.

The shift to the book as an object is tantamount to asking why this format, why this publication vehicle, why this price point, why this paper… if you truthfully answer those questions authentically, you are serving an audience. Why would my readers want this? How does this provide value to my audience? All your choices, if they are based on how you are serving your end client to their highest goal, are also answering the question of book as object and also book as communication vehicle.



This is a difficult question to answer because speaking specifically about Japanese photography, my answers will be different. And speaking about which period of time – pre-war, post-war, post-protest, contemporary – depending on the time period, the answer is different too.

I will focus just on post-war (I will say post-war is from late 1940s, short of 1949 to late 1960s, early 1970s). Writing discourse is immensely important to understand Japanese photography at that time because it is about a network of ideas and a network of people connected intra-generationally or inter-generationally. The conflict or acquiescence of those people is a network of ideas. It informs how the photographs were read, like a lattice. The photographs hang on that lattice, that discourse. The meaning, usage, the reception of those images modified over time as the language changed, and as the photographer chose a different use.

A photographer's language – and the writings of others in newspapers, journals, magazines, weeklies like *Life* or *Time*, *Life*-type publications, in independent publications, criticism, histories of, writings on, dialogues, roundtable discussions – all created an ongoing discourse. It was a process of self-identification and allegiance. "I identify with this group; I do not identify with that group" and "these are the words we use. We don't use those words", "this is how we talk about this, we do not talk about that". All of this was important because photographers were responding and creating work with that in mind.

That is where you get into a situation: how much of it is photographers making work for other photographers? That is a very relevant topic of discussion in post-war Japanese photography especially because each photographer is dealing with a lot of shared themes. After the 1970s, language and its relationship with photography is quite strong, but it is much more a conceptual, triangulated relationship rather than what it was previously, which was discourse oriented.

*What would make a better photobook ecosystem?*

That's a very nested question: are you talking about monographs and photographers who are making portfolio books and getting them out into the world? If so, I would say maybe photographers can pool their resources and have publishing clubs and build audiences and markets that way.

This is going to sound a bit harsh, but some publishing is making pretty books for people to enjoy them. By this I mean that they're very decoupled from timeliness. They are like art artefacts. It doesn't matter if it sells this year or next year or two years from now. How timely does it need to be? It is not necessary to be timely. This is maybe the first parameter in defining a market and publishing

    *Ivan Vartanian*

model. If you do or do not have urgency – where it needs to get out now. Where it doesn't matter if it comes out now or 10 years from now, if those kinds of people who are bookmakers can get together and start to powwow their business model and publishing model, that would be great. I think that probably most people who are coming to the photobook world are individual photographers looking to make their photobook. And that's what I would say to them, but that's very different from what I do.

*What's currently on your desk?*

A Garfield mug. Garfield is on a canopy and one end of it is in the teeth of Odie. The caption is "it's not a pretty life, but someone has to live it". This is from 1978. I have owned this thing since 1978. It is my favourite object in the world. Apart from an iPhone cord and my glasses, that's it on my desk. [Note to editor: One week after this interview, I dropped the mug, shattering it. The shards are assembled in a small pile that I'll memorialise in some way.]

# Buen Lugar

Buen Lugar is an independent editorial initiative that publishes photobooks and zines with a special interest in long-term projects that consider print as part of the narrative strategy. The publishing house was founded in 2014 by Aribel González, Alejando Olivares and Cristóbal Olivares. Together, they have published 18 titles.

Alejandro and Cristóbal are photographers, so I guess it is natural to think of the book as the most appropriate vehicle to mark an intention with a specific work. In 2014, we started to explore the idea of publishing our own work and at the time there were few editorial chances in Chile. Just a few photobook initiatives with no money to support everyone.

So, we thought: why don't we try to have more control over how we publish our work? That's how it started. We didn't set out with the ambition to publish others. We didn't consider ourselves editors for a long time. At the time, it was difficult to gain access to great photobooks in Chile, so it was always amazing to find one, or have a friend who travelled abroad to bring you back something. So, from there, when you gain access, the inspiration was even greater.

I remember browsing through the flea market in Santiago (Persa Bio-Bio), looking for used books or, in this case, photobooks. At that time, between 2005-09, you were still able to find photobooks from the 1970s or 80s. For example *Chile Ayer y Hoy* (1975) by Gabriela Mistral or *El infarto del alma* (1994) by Paz Errazuriz. These books today are very difficult to find, and, if you manage to do so, they are very expensive collectors' items. Obviously, I didn't know them at the time and they were not expensive either, but I just wanted to have photobooks from Chile to look at. And if you were extra lucky, you could find international photobooks that someone got tired of, or forgot about, and there it was. One day, I found a copy of the photographer Pep Bonet's book about AIDS in Africa.



It depends entirely on the quality of the work, whether it has something to say, the feel, the coherence, the timing. Not just a collection of great photos. We try to work with the author as much as we can, side-by-side. This is very, very important. Also, we ask ourselves the question of whether the photobook is the right form to put this specific work out there. Is it the right time for this work? Will they have a greater impact on specific audiences in other forms? Why print? Why us?

This is also very difficult to answer because it differs from project to project and we do not want to set a bar about what is good and what is not. But what we do want to see in a project is commitment and hard work. Not just scratches on the surface of a given topic. We want to see deeper meanings and connections. We believe in *try, try, try* – in perseverance and patience whilst doing a project. "Flight hours" and field work are important, photographically speaking of course. Very much like slow cooking.

Sometimes there are projects that need more field work. More images in the pool, more time to reflect on the theme. Or maybe an emotional distance between the author and their own images. It is hard to explain but I think publishers will relate to the experience when the team feels when it's more or less right; when everything just seems to fall in place.

Up to now, I think we mostly start a project if we get along with the author, as a team. We hardly accept a submission or proposal from someone we do not know or whose work we don't know (we do not have an open submission system). We have published photographers who have been referred or directed to us, and we get to know each other from that point. For us, it has to be about natural encounters.



We try to engage as many audiences as we can. We often do activities with public schools, explaining the process of making a book and telling the stories behind every project. It is important for us to let them know that this very specific artistic form of expression exists and they can be part of it. We talk about the editing process, the press, the design but most importantly about the stories behind the books we are presenting, including the topics, the motivations, the ideas and the behind-the-scenes, not to mention the mistakes. For us, the mistakes are a very important element; we use them as our allies, as one more element of the storytelling. We try to pass on the message that it is OK to make errors. Embrace trial and error and keep moving with what makes you feel happy. It is important for us because we (those of us at Buen Lugar) came mostly from public schools and we do know that there is sometimes no interest in the visual arts. That being said, and to be honest, I still think, as of today, that the audience for photobooks are mostly photographers, designers or artists. We are still some distance from opening that up.

It is good and bad that the audience is narrow. For example, the fact that it is such a specific audience allows us to work with more subtle and cryptic languages and resources that we know will be understood or valued, and we nourish ourselves amongst peers. But at the same time, we limit the opportunity for these types of projects to be understood in a more fluid way amongst different audiences. For this reason, we believe that the best way to make our way of working understood is through mediation, fairs, talks, schools, and so on. This way, we can explain directly to people (regardless of whether or not they are part of the photographic or artistic community) what is behind our projects, the stories we want to tell through our books and the anecdotes that serve to bring such projects to the public. But at the same time, we do need to expand the audience not only because of sales or distribution but as a cultural contribution, especially to those who might not be able to have access to culture. We keep in mind the gigantic socio-economic gap in Chile that marks our entire identity as a country.



In the photobook ecosystem specifically, the editorial format becomes an important part of the project's story. This is how our work methodology differs from the editions of other more conventional or catalogue-style books; the team works collectively and is interdisciplinary, and the design is not merely a function but an element that takes on a role that is as important as the images. The layout, typography, colour palette, paper, binding, finishing, type of printing and so on are directly related to the final perception of the story and how it is told, as well as the sensory relationship that the reader has with the book. We think of it as an experience.

We try to make it so that our books are an intimate record of someone who has something to say and wants to share an experience with an audience, to see if they feel more or less the same. Or maybe totally different? Who knows! That's the beauty of it, the dialogue. We try to make sure that every element and every decision has a meaning, and that they talk to each other and somehow make sense. When you touch it, smell it, you have your own experience. We want to leave traces of the process and not just show the triumph of the result. Also, we try to think about the materials very consciously. For example, they can vary from the handmade bound to cheap prints to fancy offset prints.

Other times, we do not have enough resources, so we have to creatively resolve a budget problem. And if there is something that could define us as independent publishers (or maybe Latin American independent publishers?), it is that we all have to try to solve it with what we have, and that creates an identity, a purpose and a statement, if you like.

*How do you attempt to address sustainability in publishing?*

We try to be as conscious as we can about that. For example, we do not publish large numbers of copies (maximum 500) and do not use too much plastic-like foils, for example. We bring this question into the mix of every book process. Also, depending on the project, we do low-scale, handmade publications, mixing suppliers and printing techniques.

*Who have been the models or templates for your own activities?*

When we started, other independent (and not so independent) editorial initiatives supported and created the scene. Amongst them, but not limited to, are Ediciones Económicas de Fotografía Chilena (an underground operation from the 1980s, but no longer active), Ediciones La Visita, FIFV Ediciones, Ocho Libros, Pehuén and LOM. We think that the initiatives that are working now owe a lot to them. They opened and paved the way for all of us here in Chile.

*What would make a better photobook ecosystem?*

We believe that if we could actually engage more audiences, instead of just talking about it, we could all benefit from it. To finally print a book is such a challenging process, so, on top of it all, to think that we also have to promote, create audiences, distribute, engage, sell, be culturally active, stay creative and so on is frightening and a very long walk to take. We love it, but it is not easy. By the time you finally have the money to print, you are almost exhausted! That's why we try to stay more or less free and try to have fun with it. We find it hard to look at it as a business and we know we are falling short in that regard. In a way, it is not a marathon for us. We prefer the walk in the park.

That being said, there are initiatives that only deal with mediations, and that's amazing. Like a fresh breeze. For example, *Imagen Salvaje*, a project led by Ana María Briede that was born from the Valparaíso International Photography Festival that specifically deals with mediations and education within communities and schools through art and photography.

*What's currently on your desk?*

A computer, plants, a printer, a film scanner, a battery charger, pens and knives, post-its, notebooks, a daily planner, a Wacom tablet, an iPhone, two books, hard drives, a cutting pad, a card reader, a Korg chromatic tuner, a small dinosaur, The Simpsons figurines.

# Sanjay Kak

Sanjay Kak is the Founder of Yaarbal Books, a publishing imprint based in New Delhi, India. At Yaarbal, he has edited and published the photobook Witness – Kashmir 1986–2016, 9 Photographers (2017) and Cups of Nun Chai (2020). He is also the editor of the anthology Until My Freedom Has Come – The New Intifada in Kashmir (Haymarket Books, 2013). As an independent documentary filmmaker, his work includes Red Ant Dream (2013), Jashn-e-Azadi ('How We Celebrate Freedom') (2007) and Words on Water (2002). A self-taught filmmaker, Sanjay has been active with the documentary cinema movement in India, and with the Cinema of Resistance project.

*What is your process for arriving at decisions about books and the projects that you undertake?*

I cannot pretend that I came into photobooks steeped in its traditions, or even those of photography. I came to the genre in an entirely instrumental way: wanting to tell a story that was not possible to tell in any other way.

*Witness – Kashmir 1986-2016, 9 Photographers* (2017), my first book as a publisher, is about Kashmir and its troubled present, described through the work of nine Kashmiri photographers. The book was released in 2017 but its roots go back to 10 years earlier, to *Jashn-e-Azadi* ('*How We Celebrate Freedom*'), a feature-length documentary film about Kashmir which I had finished in 2007. It was whilst working on this film that I chanced upon the work of some of the photojournalists whose work eventually featured in the book. I had sought out their images in an attempt to evoke the 1990s in Kashmir, a decade that began with the euphoria of a massive and popular uprising against India but was soon marked by terrible brutalities, as the state apparatus sought to re-impose its writ in ways which were unspeakably bloody, and with what were eventually fratricidal consequences. Since people were unable (or unwilling) to speak about the 90s, I wondered if I could I evoke those years more obliquely, through photography suggestive of those years.

At first, I was looking at the work of these photojournalists in a limited, evidentiary way. It was only over a period of time, that I realised that the work of this motley group, the oldest almost 60 and the youngest not yet 20, was taking a shape, and that as a collective body of work, it was telling its own story, about a generation (perhaps even two) whose lives were shaped by their photography. That is when I began to think of a photobook because I thought that it could provide a wider audience an unusual and rewarding entry into Kashmir.

Outside of the glossy, expensive coffee-table books we don't really have a very rich tradition of mainstream publishers supporting photobooks in India. Kashmir in any case is difficult political terrain for publishers, so I knew fairly early that a fat 400-page photobook was certainly not something that would find takers here. So what began as a curatorial idea gradually triggered a decision to set up Yaarbal Books, a publishing imprint with a primary focus on narratives from Kashmir, although we are obviously open to looking at other things in the future. As we got closer into the production of the book, and having understood a little bit about the limits of the book-trade in India – including the opacity of most distributors to photobooks – we also decided to distribute the book ourselves!

I will admit that my background as a documentary filmmaker in India, frequently working with narratives that were driven by the politics of our times, and my experience of not just making films independently but also distributing them, first as VHS tapes and DVD discs, and more recently as digital files, was an invaluable guide. It did make me a little less fearful about the task we were up against.

Our second publication, *Cups of Nun Chai* (2020) came out of an art project by the artist Alana Hunt. She had been working with and showing iterations of the work in art spaces in Australia for almost a decade before she decided to turn it into a book. Alana has had a long-standing engagement with Kashmir, something that began when she was a student in New Delhi in 2009. By the time she returned home in the summer of 2010, Kashmir was roiled by great unrest, and before the year was out, 118 people had been killed in protests on the streets. Alana was back in Australia by then but responded to her distress with what eventually became *Cups of Nun Chai*. It remains a very poignant work of memorialisation, constructed around conversations that she conducted around the making and drinking of nun chai, a traditional salty tea from Kashmir, which is drunk at almost any moment of the day for everyday sustenance. But it is also an essential part of hospitality, and is even served at times of mourning. Alana had turned the act of the making of nun chai into a simple gesture of remembrance for those 118 lives, and into a very compelling account of what the struggle in Kashmir was all about. The fact that she was a kind of "outsider" was no disadvantage, and in fact gave her conversations a special edge, for she was able to draw a relationship between state control and violence in Kashmir with those in other parts of the world. Whilst this text was absolutely critical, her pictures of these encounters also formed an important part of the project: always the same deceptively simple top-angle shot of each one of the 118 cups. Eventually these accounts appeared in a local newspaper in Kashmir, the *Kashmir Reader*, so in a sense the memorial had reached home.

Perhaps because she had seen *Witness*, Alana reached out asking if there was a possible book in the materials she had been showing in galleries. And there certainly was.

     *Sanjay Kak*

I think my way of working is shaped by my background in filmmaking. In documentary, I learnt to approach the work as an ensemble act, where what we call the "filmmaker" is only one amongst a larger cohort who help shape a film – and this includes the cinematographer, sound recordist, editor, musician, sound-mixer, colour-grader and so on. I'm not down-playing the central role of the director figure, but just acknowledging that the others are as crucial in helping find a way through the material, in even telling us what we may be looking for. I can say without hesitation that the best moments in my film work have come when I have been able to sense that someone in the crew has independently detected a new strand in the material, something otherwise unexpressed, and then my role has been to help them find a way to bring it home.

For *Witness*, I found much of the process of bookmaking to be analogous to putting together a film – except that you could say that I was working with what we could call the "found footage" of nine different cameramen! In making the shift to the photobook, there was a new skill-set that had to be located but I could see that those skills had ready parallels in film. We had camera-people in both, but the role of the film editor had its equivalence in the photo editors as well as the designers, the colourist was played by the printing supervisors, and of course the offset printers stood in for the old film-processing laboratories or the later post-production studios.

Some of the relationships that underlay *Witness* are very old and well-worked out ones. I have worked with designer Itu Chaudhuri for almost 35 years, from the days when he made artworks for our film titles, pasting them by hand, letter by letter. But there was also a younger cohort who came to the task with a richer sense of contemporary photography (as well as of the photobook) and I have no doubt that their inputs played a part in the shape that the book eventually took. We had the counsel of two accomplished photojournalists: Ishan Tankha, who is himself now a photobook maker, helped in editing down the longlist of pictures, and Kaushik Ramaswamy, who prepared the images and supervised the printing. And there was Sukanya Baskar from Itu Chaudhuri Design too, who was fresh out of design school at the time and did the hands-on work of designing every page. I must add that New Delhi has developed a vibrant scene around photography and photobooks in recent years. So there is something like a community that you can call in on, for both aesthetic and technical responses, as well as printing presses that are alert to the needs of such work, so that you do not ever feel that you are completely on your own.

With *Cups of Nun Chai*, I was more like a producer of a film, even if I was a fairly active and opinionated one! It was not easy to work on a book with a dispersed workforce: Alana Hunt in Australia, Itu Chaudhuri Design in one part of Delhi and me in another. What helped was that Alana already had most of the material and knew it well. She also started with a very good sense of what the book should be like. I remember one of the earliest conversations that we had together as a triad, where she said she wanted a book that looked and felt like a paperback, which you could toss into your bag, and read on the bus or metro. She wanted to steer clear of anything that smelt of precious, not just in the size and design but also down to the paper we would be printing on.

I find the offset process very satisfying. Given that our print runs for both books were not massive, we ended up using machines that were not the newest, hopelessly automated monsters. I think that was a blessing because it required something more tactile from us, and the process became almost artisanal, what with the machine operator, the Ustad, the boss that he was, constantly making tiny tweaks to the settings, and the almost esoteric way in which he often physically masked sections of the plates to achieve a desired effect. That translation from a digital file on a screen to a digital proof, and from that to what is finally rolling off the offset printing machine is nerve-wracking but also exhilarating! The fact that we had to physically stand there for two whole weeks and sign-off on each plate always gave me an unexpected rush of pleasure!

*How do you balance choices between working with highly specific materials or processes, and the desire for access?*

I think the earliest brief that the designers had for *Witness* was that it was a kind of repository, an archive that held the visual memory of 30 years of Kashmir's contemporary history. From quite early on we thought of it as a kind of folder, but a substantial one, something that demanded time and attention from the reader, not at all casual. It was also meant to suggest something that if not permanent, was at least long-lasting. That demanded appropriate paper, and its grammage in turn opened up the possibilities of how adventurous we could be with the production. These decisions were taken almost simultaneously with the design, and we actually conducted small tests on different kinds of paper, and this was long before we were producing various sets of dummies. It allowed us to think of a certain scale, and create the place for over 200 photographs. The physical characteristics – paper, size and so on – also allowed us to build in what I sometimes call the performative elements of the design. There are strings to unravel before you open the book, gatefolds that open up in unconventional ways, postcards that drop out of the book and so on.

I think good design can make a book feel more expensive than it actually is. By which I mean that some sort of early clarity about materials and processes helps a great deal. I referred to Alana's desire to have *Cups of Nun Chai* have the feel of a paperback. She would have ideally liked it to have been printed on newsprint, and we did run some tests on what passes as newsprint here in India but the feedback was not at all reassuring. The eventual decision to print it on very ordinary bulk paper helped because that is what paperback novels are printed on in India. And once you know what the characteristics of your paper are, you know how you need to prepare your images, what the outer limits of how they will reproduce colours are and what the blacks are going to be like. All that helps keep the design process on an even keel so that there are no late surprises at the very end.

Whilst I'm stressing the need to plan ahead and anticipate the direction of the book, I think it's probably as important to be alert to last minute possibilities. With *Witness*, I can think of two fairly late interventions that had a major impact on how the book works. The first had to do with how the pictures were annotated, with us constantly trimming the word length of the descriptions that were set below each image until we had arrived at the very minimal "feather captions" that worked best for the layout of the pictures and the overall design. But there was this nagging doubt that in this paring down the more archival dimension of these pictures was getting diluted. That is when Itu Chaudhuri suggested we add a section at the back of the book, a sort of yellow-pages where every single image was described in some detail, down to what stock it had been shot on, arranged chronologically and with a thumbnail image. It was a lot of work, especially since it came in the last weeks of production. But even if these yellow-pages are not the first thing you notice when you pick-up the book, I know it is something that gives the book a real, solid archival dimension.

The other decision that was taken at the very last minute, when we had almost gone to press with the insides of the book was probably much more critical: what did the book look like before you opened it? We had played with various options of fairly severe looking "archive" boxes, mostly in black, but somehow they all seemed to signal "limited edition art-project". Whereas what we were really after was a book, the kind that bookshops could stock on their shelves. Once again it was Itu Chaudhuri who came up with the idea of something that looked like a "*sarkari*" folder, an official binder, the kind that we are familiar with in India. These are usually wrapped in red cloth and tied up with thick white string, so that is what we eventually developed: an open spine for the book, a binding in red cloth and a white string that was wrapped around the book.

*What is the public for a photobook? Who do you think of as your audience?*

The photobook is still a niche thing in India, and there are many reasons for that, with the relatively high cost of production being one inevitable factor. So the aspiration for *Witness*, which is a 400-page book (and weighing in at 1.5 kg), cannot be that it will turn into a best-seller in the marketplace. But if it strikes a chord with the reader the audience can be quite unexpected. In Kashmir, people turned to the book as a kind of intimate archive, something that contains memories that have otherwise been systematically effaced, and this included ordinary images that have turned out to have extraordinary valency today (I'm thinking, for example, of the very first image in the book, from Kashmir in 1986, where a group of activists are marching in support of Palestine!). In India, *Witness* has made its way into bookstores all across the country, and continues to be sold, a few copies at a time, but steadily. It has also entered into spaces where photography and photobooks are valued, and that includes the art space. I value those points of entry because it brings Kashmir to new audiences. Difficult conversations will never be invited into the living room through the front door, so we must look for the opportunity to inveigle ourselves in whichever way is possible. I have myself travelled extensively with *Witness*, doing book talks in dozens of universities, both in the US and UK. Selling copies of the book at these events is important, and we always do that, but the space that it creates for a conversation is as important. At these events, I use the book in an almost performative way, unwrapping its different facets, projecting some of the images, reading first-person bits from the photographers and so on.

In 2020, we were invited to show the book – as a book, not just as a collection of photographs – at the Sydney Biennale. So we created an environment inside a gallery space that literally opened the book out to a completely new and unexpected audience. What was also amazing was that the curators had also arranged for a set of images from *Witness* to be blown up on huge vinyls that were stretched across various structures on Cockatoo Island in Sydney Harbour, the central venue of the Biennale. That year, the Sydney Biennale was sadly overtaken by Covid-19 the week it opened, so that was a real blow.

With *Cups of Nun Chai*, we began by printing a limited number of copies, and assumed that it would have its audience mostly in Australia, where Alana lived and worked, with probably a little spillover here in India. But it has actually done very well in India, and despite the fact that it came out during the pandemic and that we have hardly had any resources to promote it, the book has gone into a reprint. I'm sure that Alana has had similar experiences in Australia but I know that when she was briefly here in New Delhi, the public events around the book were deeply impactful. I can recall a very intense interaction with students at the School of Arts & Aesthetics at Jawaharlal Nehru University in Delhi, and where Alana was once a student, at a time when the university was going through a very challenging, restrictive time, and it became an occasion to break the silence around Kashmir in a very powerful way. We also had a great conversation at the Offset Projects space in Okhla, Delhi, where she was engaging with a much more diverse set of arts practitioners. Each time the presence of the book made possible a very nuanced conversation around Kashmir, around how artists can (and must) respond to crises, and about the nature of art practice itself.

As a filmmaker who worked with what can broadly be called political themes, I have always believed that a film can become the pivot around which an audience can be created, not just found. So can the photobook…

I don't know if there can be any rules or constraints in these matters.
A documentary can have wall-to-wall commentary, another can have
hundreds of title cards to move the narrative forward, and a third could
have neither. Yet each one can be a brilliant film because a particular
choice has been made to work. I would carry over the same yardstick
to the photobook: what does it need? Are the photographs alone
telling the story I want to tell? Is the edit and layout and design
conveying enough? And does the addition of text, or captions, or end
notes, add or take away from the power of the photographs? It's
answers to these questions that will help us decide, and not some
abstract code of conduct.

In *Witness*, I decided to add a sort of profile at the end of each
photographer's images, written up from the many conversations
I had with them in the course of curating the book. Those texts were
an intrusion into the book, but it allowed some degree of access into
the lives of these nine men, and into what brought them into image
making. (Sadly there are no women in that cohort, because at the time
the book was made, there were no women photojournalists practicing
in Kashmir. Several have since come up, and they are really good.)
In a sense, these conversations provided a reflective space for what
it means to grow up within a conflict, and why some sought out
photography as a way of finding their way through it, and finally, how
the practice of individuals has changed and shifted over the years.
There is a kind of sociology there that I am personally very interested
in, and was hoping that others would be too.

In the case of *Cups of Nun Chai*, the 118 conversations are what
the book is really about, and the images of the individual cups only
strike a kind of ritual posture for each of the texts. I see it as a book
of 118 bits of prose set up to look like a photobook! That is what the
design of the book also achieves, in that it is enormously attentive
to the text, but the simple, almost repetitive tone struck by the
photographs plays an enormous part in keeping them together,
for the book to cohere.

      *Sanjay Kak*

Is it arrogant to say that one does not have any role models? I certainly have inspirations but those are at the grandest level. For example, in cinema I have felt truly lifted by the work of Andrei Tarkovsky, and in a different way by the documentary work of Harun Farocki. I greatly admire the writing of Eduardo Galeano. Although my own work can hardly be said to be modelled on the work of any of these artists, I do know that exposure to their ways of thinking has shaped the way I am. From my own practice as a filmmaker in India, and as someone who has been involved in the practice of circulating films, of helping create a screening culture, I have learnt a lot about what role films, books and culture more generally can be. So as a book-maker I look towards my comrades in the Cinema of Resistance in India, as well as the Peoples Film Collective. I'm not a fan of the art gallery, of the white cube, which I see as an insulated and somewhat cold space.

*What would make a better photobook ecosystem?*

As someone who is working in India at a very worrying time, when we have already gone through a massive swing towards the right, towards a crude majoritarianism and a dumbing down of all intellectual endeavour, what I crave most is the space in which to show young people what the alternatives are. We need spaces to show them films, we need bookshops to sell books they need to read, we need libraries where they can read and watch things. That is the world that I would like to see photobooks stepping into, becoming a part of the resistance to mediocrity.

# Anastasiia Leonova

Anastasiia Leonova is a publisher, art manager, curator, and co-founder of ist publishing based in Ukraine. Between 2014-20, she ran an independent art gallery in Kharkiv focused on contemporary art. With a background in Sociology and Art History, she specialises in photography and photobooks. Leonova is the curator of Mystetska Biblioteka, a project promoting contemporary artistic editions, and runs The Naked Books, a Kyiv-based shop dedicated to artistic books. She founded BOOK CHAMPIONS WEEKEND, a festival for photobook publishers, in 2021, and served on the jury for the 2023 Dummy Book Award.

At ist publishing, we approach each book not just as a physical object but as the heart of a larger conversation. Publishing is a long-term journey – a process that extends into exhibitions, presentations, book signings, and the dialogues these encounters spark. To make this journey meaningful, we prioritise collaboration with artists whose practices we've followed over time. This allows us to build mutual trust, ensuring that both the artist and the publisher are aligned upon navigating the unpredictable yet rewarding path of bookmaking.

But book publishing is never just about aesthetics or storytelling. The decision to publish is often driven by urgency – political, social and cultural. Right now, in Ukraine, this urgency is sharpened by the context of war. Many of our projects focus on war-related topics, both in artistic and theoretical realms. These themes are not just relevant, but crucial. They help us process and accept our collective and individual experiences, offering a lens through which we can confront the realities of our time.

Take, for example, works that highlight resilience, embody a sense of mission, or contribute to the ongoing narrative of nation-building during times of profound upheaval. *Saints* (2024) by Sasha Maslov is one such book. This photobook shares the profound personal sacrifices made by Ukrainians during the Russian invasion of 2022-23. Through over 100 photographs and stories, Maslov portrays soldiers in the Armed Forces, volunteers and civilians whose everyday efforts contribute to Ukraine's defence efforts. It is a work that speaks to the essence of modern sanctity – a concept redefined by the selflessness and resilience of ordinary people during the decade-long war.

Before 2022, we primarily focused on artistic projects and rarely worked with documentary photography. But nowadays, timing has become everything. With *Saints*, it felt like an urgent need to tell these stories to the world. We produced this 320-page book in a record four months, working through relentless shelling and constant power outages. The result was nothing short of extraordinary, with more than 2000 copies pre-sold before going to print. In peaceful times, I could never have imagined such a scenario, but this experience demonstrated the power of photobooks as more than just artistic representation. They are also a vital tool for information, a means of communicating urgent, real-world narratives that demand to be heard.

Of course, we'd be remiss not to acknowledge the financial realities that shape this work. The cost of producing photobooks has risen sharply, and securing funding is more difficult than ever. Selling them presents its own challenges – photobooks exist in a niche market with high prices, where distributors often take more than half the revenue. At times, it feels like photobook publishing will remain the domain of the truly devoted. And yes, we proudly count ourselves amongst them.

Still, commercial considerations inevitably play a role. If an artist has a grant, a partner institution willing to support the project or a dedicated audience eager to purchase the book, it naturally becomes a higher priority. These partnerships and opportunities enable us to keep the doors open for projects that might otherwise remain unrealised.

For us, every book we publish is a commitment – not just to the artist, but to the audience and the questions that define our moment. Whether it's a local story in Ukraine or a conversation about war, memory and identity, our goal is to create books that transcend their pages, sparking the kind of engagement that can reshape how we see and understand the world.

*How do you like to work with people?*

For each book we create, we assemble a unique team of translators, editors, designers, and printers tailored to the specific project and its demands. Every publication has its own vision and challenges, and we believe the right collaboration is key to bringing it to life. That said, we also have a trusted pool of professionals – people whose work we've relied on for years and who understand our ethos.

As a publisher, I'm fully immersed in art direction. From the careful selection of works and the crafting of sequences to overseeing the precision of printing proofs, I ensure that every detail aligns with the vision of the book. When it comes to photobooks, the collaboration between designer and artist is particularly crucial. The designer must not only have technical expertise but also a deep connection to the artist's work and a sensitivity to its nuances. This relationship often involves close teamwork under tight conditions, requiring trust, open communication and a shared creative language. Our process is deeply collaborative, with every book serving as the culmination of many perspectives and efforts, creating something both meaningful and enduring.

When an artist approaches us to create a book together, I believe they come with certain expectations – of quality, care and the level of visibility we've built through our previous projects. It's a trust we take seriously, and we strive to maintain that standard with every publication.

However, delivering on that promise is a nuanced challenge. On one hand, we're deeply committed to honouring the artist's vision, ensuring the book reflects their expectations and creative intentions. On the other, we must navigate the realities of the book market. This means making the work accessible – both in terms of pricing and presentation – to the audience that has trusted us for years.

It's a delicate balance, blending artistic ambition with practical considerations. The goal is always the same: to create a book that not only stands as a testament to the artist's work but also finds its place in the hands of readers who will appreciate and connect with it. The challenge is what makes it rewarding – crafting something that resonates on multiple levels, staying true to our ethos whilst continuously adapting to an ever-changing landscape.



Photobooks have long existed in a niche space – a specialised audience of other photographers, publishers, collectors, enthusiasts, and art-world professionals who gather at book fairs, enter contests and celebrate their craft in awards. This ecosystem is vibrant, but it is also insular. The question we constantly grapple with is how to expand this audience, to bring photobooks out of the art bubble and into the hands of a broader public. And should we really expand it?

Last year, this question took on a new urgency when we were approached by Ukraine's largest electricity provider, which supplies 90% of the country's power. After suffering catastrophic losses to infrastructure during the brutal winter of 2022-23 – when Russian missile strikes and shelling damaged countless energy facilities and left millions in the dark – they wanted to create something remarkable. At first glance, this collaboration seemed unusual. What does a power company have to do with photobooks? Yet, for us, it was a natural fit.

We drew on our extensive network of photographers, many of whom risked their lives to document the fallout of this energy crisis. The resulting book is a powerful visual story of resilience, featuring work by more than 30 Ukrainian photographers. It is a tribute to those who refused to give up – engineers and electricians who worked tirelessly to ensure that darkness didn't prevail.

For me, this project was, in a certain way, a revelation. It proved that photobooks can transcend their origins. They can become tools of storytelling and education, reaching audiences far beyond the art world. Making photobooks more accessible is not just an artistic challenge but a communicative one. By bridging the gap between the photobook community and the broader book market, we can amplify their impact. Photobooks may have started in a niche, but they don't have to remain there. It's not just about expanding the audience, but expanding the possibilities of what a photobook can be.



Photobooks, by their very nature, present invaluable opportunities for cross-cultural learning. The ability to make such works accessible worldwide reinforces their significance – not just for the communities they originate from, but for the global conversation they can enrich. When shared with a wider audience, even the most specific stories begin to reveal their connections to shared human experiences, transforming them into universal reflections.

Often, projects like the ones we work on in Ukraine focus on deeply local topics, yet they hold universal relevance when viewed through a global context. Take, for instance, our latest photobook, *The Chips: Ukrainian Naïve Mosaics of the 1950-90s* (2024), by Yevgen Nikiforov and Polina Baitsym. This work documents the fragile beauty of mosaics created by unknown authors – a vanishing phenomenon in public art and memory. Although these mosaics are specific to Ukraine, the theme resonates far beyond the country's borders, echoing the preservation challenges faced by similar public art forms in the UK, Mexico and India.

At ist publishing, our efforts extend beyond photobooks. We are deeply committed to translating and publishing texts in philosophy, anthropology, architecture and other culturally relevant fields. By bringing thinkers such as W.G. Sebald, Rem Koolhaas, Anna Tsing,

     *Anastasiia Leonova*

John Berger, and Susan Sontag into the Ukrainian context, we aim to bridge intellectual gaps that often leave us isolated from the broader international dialogue. Like any book, a photobook is fundamentally an act of communication – an exchange across geographies and cultures. It is a way to address the distances that separate us whilst uncovering shared dilemmas we all face, even if our engagement with those dilemmas differs.

What makes this effort so compelling is the recognition that photobook publishers from all corners of the globe face strikingly similar challenges in the photobook market. Rising production costs, small audiences and the precarious nature of distribution are universal obstacles. However, these shared difficulties highlight the vitality of the photobook as a medium. The struggle to preserve and disseminate these unique cultural artefacts is not an isolated endeavour but part of a broader global effort to connect, communicate and understand one another in ways that transcend language, borders and time.

The global network of publishers, artists and readers, each grappling with similar questions and concerns, becomes a testament to the enduring power of the book as a shared cultural venture. Bringing a photobook to another continent is not merely about extending its reach, but itself act of profound understanding.

*What is the place of language and writing in a book of photographs?*

Language is a bridge, a foundation for communication that connects the visual and the textual, offering context, meaning and dialogue. For me, it is a vital part of any book.

In Ukraine, the role of language has become even more charged during Russia's full-scale invasion. For decades, our society existed in a bilingual state, a cultural legacy of imperial influence (roughly half of Ukrainians spoke Russian, whilst the other half spoke Ukrainian). There was something beautiful about this coexistence – friends sitting at the same table, speaking in two languages without even switching, effortlessly blending them in a way that fostered mutual understanding.

But the war changes everything. Many of us came to realise that speaking Russian was not entirely their choice but a legacy of imposed dominance, a remnant of cultural erasure carefully engineered over centuries. This realisation sparked a nationwide shift, an intentional decision to reclaim Ukrainian as a language of daily life, resistance and identity.

At first, it was difficult. Language isn't just about grammar; it's deeply personal. It carries memories, habits and intimacy. For many, the transition was most challenging with loved ones, where a shared vocabulary of affection – specific words, familiar intonations – had been forged in Russian. But with time, speaking Ukrainian has become second nature, a habit that carried weight and meaning, a step toward preserving and nourishing something truly ours.

In our photobooks, this relationship with language finds expression through a dual-language approach. Each book speaks in Ukrainian, honouring its local roots, and in English, opening its narrative to the world. This balance feels right: it respects the images, the stories they tell and the audiences who will hold these books in their hands.

*Who have been the models or templates for your own activities?*

The guiding lights of my work are many, each offering something invaluable. Loose Joints inspires with their bold, fresh selection of projects, daring to venture where others might hesitate. Spector Books captivates with its exceptional design, turning every page into a tactile experience that enhances the narrative. Images Vevey stands out for their thoughtful and caring collaboration with artists, creating a space where creativity thrives in mutual respect. Jason Eskenazi's wisdom on photo sequencing has been a treasure, teaching me that the order of images is as powerful as the images themselves. Antoine d'Agata, with his boundless enthusiasm for creating new books and reinvigorating the methods of presenting work, continually pushes me to think beyond conventional boundaries. And, of course, all of our authors, who, through each project, show me how to look deeper, to resist rushing toward conclusions, and to embrace the raw truth of the story without unnecessary interpretations.

*What would make a better photobook ecosystem?*

A better photobook ecosystem is one that addresses the economic challenges and distribution hurdles faced by publishers, artists and

     *Anastasiia Leonova*

readers alike. The photobook, as an art form and a medium of storytelling, thrives in a specialised ecosystem, but to grow and become more accessible, we need to rethink how it is produced, sold and shared across the globe.

One of the most pressing issues in the photobook world is financial sustainability. The production of photobooks, particularly those that involve high-quality printing, binding, and design, is expensive. As costs continue to rise – driven by inflation, the increasing price of materials and labour shortages – many small publishers are forced to make difficult decisions about the number of copies they can print or the price they must charge. This creates a barrier to entry for new publishers, limits the variety of voices in the market, and, in some cases, forces publishers to choose between maintaining artistic integrity and ensuring the financial viability of a project.

To address this, publishers, artists and distributors need to build more collaborative financial models. This could involve pooling resources for shared production costs, offering crowd-funding opportunities for specific projects, or working with larger institutions – such as museums, galleries or cultural organisations – that can help fund photobook projects whilst offering wider visibility. It is also important to reconsider how photobooks are priced. Whilst they are often considered niche objects, pricing should strike a balance between making them accessible to a broader audience and supporting the value of the artist's work. Special editions, smaller print runs and flexible pricing models can help achieve this.

Distribution is equally important in creating a more vibrant photobook ecosystem. Currently, photobooks are primarily sold through limited markets – specialised bookstores, art galleries, photography fairs, and direct sales from publishers. These platforms are vital, but they limit the reach of photobooks to a relatively small audience. To truly expand the photobook's influence, it needs to be integrated into larger book markets, accessible in mainstream bookstores, and available through online retail platforms where a broader audience can discover them.

However, as I said, the move towards mainstream distribution must not come at the cost of artistic integrity or the community that has sustained photobooks for decades. The challenge is finding a way to expand their reach without diluting their cultural and artistic value. For this, hybrid distribution models should be explored, by partnering with online platforms or larger book retailers whilst also maintaining the intimacy of smaller, independent channels where the spirit of the photobook community thrives.

An often overlooked but critical aspect of a stronger photobook ecosystem is the need for effective marketing and promotion. Photobooks often rely on a niche audience that already understands the value of the medium. However, to grow this audience, publishers need to develop strategies that can introduce the medium to a wider public.

Lastly, a robust, transparent distribution network that ensures the availability of photobooks at multiple price points and in diverse regions is necessary. Working with distributors who understand the unique nature of photobooks and can support their presence in non-traditional retail environments (like pop-up shops, festivals and temporary exhibitions) is key to growing the ecosystem. By building more collaborative and accessible financial structures, expanding distribution beyond niche markets and investing in the promotion and education of new audiences, we can create a more sustainable and vibrant future for photobooks that is both economically viable and artistically enriching.

     *Anastasiia Leonova*

# Afterword
## Tim Clark

*Tim Clark is Editor in Chief of 1000 Words. Alongside the magazine, he is also Artistic Director for Fotografia Europea in Reggio Emilia, Italy, together with Walter Guadagnini and Luce Lebart. He has previously been involved in a wide range of projects including Curator for the Discovery section of Photo London 2022 and 2023 and Adjunct Curator on Masculinities: Liberation through Photography (2020–22) at the Barbican Centre London, an exhibition which travelled to Gropius-Bau, Berlin, Les Rencontres d'Arles and FOMU Antwerp. He teaches at The Institute of Photography, Falmouth University.*

Marking the third book in a trilogy that examines contexts for engaging with contemporary photography, *Photobook Conversations* has shifted its point of emphasis from the role or function of individuals engaged in certain forms of cultural production – as is the case with the other titles in the series *Curator Conversations* and *Writer Conversations* – to encompass multiple positions within the field of activity that is photobook publishing. Artists, editors, designers, art directors, librarians, collectors, educators, and, of course, publishers have been consulted for their critical outlooks and perspectives on the ecosystem which supports such varied and vital work. What emerges through this kaleidoscopic view is a picture of a highly creative and socially aware, international photobook community (featured here are members of the scene from Melbourne to Buenos Aires, Accra to Milan, Kathmandu to Tokyo, Kharkiv to New York). So too does a sense of profound generosity in working together to support and to share the fruits of photographers' authorship as projects go out from the studio into the world.

Photobooks remain a primary vehicle for photographers to communicate their ideas and visions, offering more experience than encounter. Amidst a world increasingly out of balance, photobooks can provide an alternative archive of representation, an empowering invitation, a place of refuge, a protective mantle, an act of resistance. They are, as Valentina Abenavoli noted in her interview, an anchor as our lives become increasingly digital and ephemeral. They also hold weight in both our personal memories and collective history. It is with tremendous gratitude and pleasure that *1000 Words* is able to publish the powerful reflections contained within these pages, insights that have been carefully garnered by editors Ana Casas Broda, Anshika Varma and Duncan Wooldridge who have worked tirelessly and diligently in selecting people to participate in the book and in conceptualising its structure, advising on texts and fostering much dialogue in the process.

     Tim Clark

We would like to acknowledge
The School of Digital Arts at Manchester
School of Art, Manchester Metropolitan
University, Hydra + Fotografía and
Offset Projects for supporting this
research. Thanks also to Lucy Soutter,
David Penny, Sylvia Waltering, Esther
Lisk-Carew, Christopher Fox, Jillian
Griffiths, Javier Godoy, Federico Estol,
Laura Laverne, Luciana Molisani and
Kirsty Fairclough.

Editors Ana Casas Broda, Anshika Varma
& Duncan Wooldridge
Series Editor Tim Clark
Copy Editor Alessandro Merola
Production Assistant Thomas King
Art Direction & Design Sarah Boris
Printed and bound in Great Britain
by Clays Ltd, Elcograf S.p.A

1000 Words
29 The Arthaus, 205 Richmond Road
London, E8 3FF, United Kingdom
info@1000wordsmag.com
www.1000wordsmag.com

ISBN 978-1-0369-0147-9



First published by 1000 Words
Photography Ltd, 2025

Distribution

UK and Europe

Public Knowledge Books
90 Hoe Street, London
E17 4QS, United Kingdom
www.publicknowledgebooks.com
bryony@publicknowledgebooks.com

North America

ARTBOOK | D.A.P.
75 Broad Street Suite 630
New York, NY 10004, US
www.artbook.com
orders@dapinc.com

Australia and New Zealand

Perimeter Distribution
734 High Street Thornbury
3071 Melbourne Victoria, Australia
www.perimeterdistribution.com
hello@perimeterdistribution.com

*Photobook Conversations* is edited by
Ana Casas Broda (Hydra + Fotografía),
Anshika Varma (Offset Projects) and
Duncan Wooldridge (Manchester
Metropolitan University). Sitting
alongside *Writer Conversations* (1000
Words, 2023), edited by Lucy Soutter
(University of Westminster) and Duncan
Wooldridge (Manchester Metropolitan
University) and *Curator Conversations*
(1000 Words, 2021), edited by Tim Clark,
it completes the trilogy of publications
exploring photography and mediation
through exhibition making, critical
writing and publishing practices.